AF553700

MENTAL RETARDATION

EDUCATION AND REHABILITATION SERVICES

ENCYCLOPAEDIA OF SPECIAL EDUCATION - VII

MENTAL RETARDATION

EDUCATION AND REHABILITATION SERVICES

By

Dr. G. Lokanadha Reddy
Dean, School of Education and
HRD and Dean Academic Affairs
Dravidian University
Kuppam - 517 426
Chittoor Dist, AP State
(India)

Dr. J. Sujathamalini
Lecturer
Avinashilingam Deemed University
Coimbatore (India)

&

Dr. A. Kusuma
M.Sc., M.Ed., M.Phil., P.G. Dip. in Statistics, Ph.D.
Dept. of Human Development and Family Studies
Sri Padmavathi Mahila Visvavidyalayam
Tirupati (A.P.)
(India)

DISCOVERY PUBLISHING HOUSE PVT. LTD.
NEW DELHI-110 002

Published by:
Namit Wasan
DISCOVERY PUBLISHING HOUSE PVT. LTD.
4383/4B, Ansari Road, Darya Ganj
New Delhi-110 002 (India)
Phone : +91-11-23279245; 23253475; 43596065
E-mail : discoverybooksindia@gmail.com
discoverypublishinghouse@gmail.com
namitwasan9@gmail.com
web : www.discoverypublishinggroup.com

Edition: **2020**

ISBN: 978-93-5056-518-6 (Set)

ISBN: 978-81-7141-786-5

Mental Retardation: ***Education and Rehabilitation Services***

Printed at:
Infinity Imaging Systems
Delhi

Foreword

Education is the fundamental right of citizens of India irrespective of their caste, creed and religion. The same is applicable to the children with abilities and disabilities. In Western world, a good literature in the form of books, identification and assessment tools, well structured and organised educational programmes and rehabilitation services are available for individuals with abilities and disabilities. In India, such things are scanty, and people are not aware of the needs of special children and even the available programmes are not reaching the needy. There are very few books dealing with special needs, especially children with mental deficiencies.

The book in your hands " Mental Retardation: Education and Rehabilitation Services" is written by Dr. G.Lokanadha Reddy, Mrs. J. Sujathamalini and Dr. A. Kusuma. The authors made a very good attempt to explain the concept of mental retardation, causes, characteristics, identification and assessment of mental retardation, education and training programmes for different categories of mentally retarded children. Further, career education, vocational rehabilitation and counseling services are discussed in detail, in this book. The rich experiences and competencies of the authors gained through their interactions in the education of children with special needs at the University of Wales Swansea, U.K. are reflected in this valuable work.

This book is highly useful to the field functionaries dealing with the mentally retarded individuals. In academic and research side, this book will be of immense value and helpful to the teachers, researchers, students and counsellors right from primary to University level. The aforesaid target group will find this book very useful and interesting to gain insight about the concept of mental retardation in education and rehabilitation services. I hope this book will give the teachers and students the pertinent intellectual and practical skills needed to work with the mentally retarded individuals.

Dr. S. MOHAN

Professor and Head
Department of Education
Alagappa University
Karaikudi.

Preface

This book is one of the several books already available in the field of Mental Retardation and we are not claiming that the material is on our own and original. But the novel feature of this book is its mode of approach to the various topics involved in the field of Mental Retardation. We do not claim any originality but for the style and method of approach. It is our earnest endeavour to expound the essentials for the subject matter as a result of our own study and experiences in special education.

There are very good number of books and manuals available for mental retardation in Western world and in India too, here and there, few books are available. But unfortunately, books which are providing comprehensive outlook on different aspects of mental retardation from concept to causes, characteristics, identification and assessment, educational programmes, social development, career education, vocational rehabilitation and counselling services are very scanty in Indian situation. We made an attempt to fill this gap through this book. In preparing this book, we have quoted and adopted some test materials from western (Seguin Form Board Test, Gessell's Developmental Schedule, Behaviour Rating Scale of AAMR) as well as Indian works (NIMH Developmental Screening Test, Vineland Social Maturity Scale—Indian Adaptation by Dr. A.J. Malin, Developmental Screening Test—Bharatraj). We are greatly acknowledging the contribution of these works in preparation of this book. And we are confident that providing all relevant information in one place will facilitate the academics, researchers and field practitioners to serve better for mentally retarded people.

The first chapter of this book deals with the concept of special education and mental retardation, definition, classification and prevalence of mental retardation. In the second chapter, factors, causes and associated problems of mental retardation apart from preventive measures are discussed. Cognitive and personality characteristics of mentally retarded children are also clearly explained in this chapter. In chapter- III, an attempt has been made to present the different tests available in the field of mental retardation for assessing the general intelligence, adaptive behaviour, specific abilities and deficits. This chapter also presents different aspects to be kept in mind in assessment of mental retardation and intervention strategies. In explaining the early intervention strategies the activities that are suggested by NIMH, Hyderabad (Mental Retardation—A Manual for Psychologists, 1989) is adopted. We greatly acknowledge NIMH for this contribution.

The educational provisions for different categories of mentally retarded, the instructional strategies and techniques used to promote desirable behaviour in mentally retarded are discussed in chapter-IV. Likewise, social development in mentally retarded children has been discussed from learning theory and developmental theory perspectives. Various intervention strategies for developing social competence in mentally retarded children are also explained in this chapter. Career education models such as School based career education model (Clark, 1979), Life centred competency based model (Brolin, 1978) and Experience based career education models (Larson 1982) for exceptional children are explained in the last chapter. Vocational rehabilitation services for mentally retarded and counselling services for parents and community are also given in this chapter.

We hope that this book will meet the requirements of teachers, teacher trainees, research scholars, counsellors and field workers at all levels of education and rehabilitation programmes. The book has other interesting features like chapter learning objectives that state what the readers should be able to after reading the chapter and a summary that recaps the main points at the end of each chapter. We do not know to what extent we have succeeded in our attempt, but we feel rewarded if this book can promote to understand the different aspects of mental retardation in children. The constructive suggestions on this book will always be welcome and greatly acknowledged.

Finally, we thank M/s Discovery Publishing House, New Delhi for the interest and promptness they have evinced in publishing this book.

—Authors

Contents

1

Concept of Mental Retardation

OBJECTIVES

This chapter deals about the concept, meaning and importance of mental retardation. It also provides various definitions of mental retardation, classification of mental retardation and prevalence of mental retardation. After reading this chapter the reader is able to understand:

1. The concept, meaning and importance of mental retardation;
2. Definitions of mental retardation;
3. Classification of mental retardation;
4. Prevalence of mental retardation.

Introduction

In a democratic country every individual has the right to education. Education moulds the individual's personality and makes them not to remain as a parasite on society. Realising this, the Government of India have introduced education as one of the fundamental rights of every individual. To provide this fundamental right to every citizen irrespective of caste, creed, religion and community etc., both the Central and State Governments have introduced many programmes such as formal education, non-formal education, informal education, adult education etc. But even after 50 years of independence, the Government of India has not achieved the objective of Universalisation of Elementary Education/Primary Education.

The reason being the high rate of wastage and stagnation particularly among the children coming from the deprived sections of the communities such as SC and ST. Further, the wastage and stagnation is also high in rural and urban slums. In a country like India where poverty, ignorance and illiteracy are dominating one can observe children with non-enrolment into the schools.

In most of the schools the teacher-student ratio is more than 1:40 and in single teacher schools the teacher is forced to handle more than one class at a time. Even there are double teacher schools, the student teacher ratio is also the same with handling of multiple classes and subjects. This makes the teacher unable to pay any individual attention and recognize the individual needs of each student. In any classroom, he or she is aiming instruction keeping in mind the average student. Thus the needs of the below average and the above average students which constitute the 40 per cent of the population, are unmet in regular classrooms in Indian situation. All the above factors are the potential contributors for dropouts, wastage and stagnation in Indian situation.

Even though the constitution of India is providing education as the fundamental right to all Indian citizens, certain groups such as pupil with physical disabilities (hearing impaired, visually impaired and orthopaedically handicapped) and mental disabilities (mental retardation) are not provided with adequate facilities to utilize this fundamental right. The reason being the normal schools existing in rural and urban areas are not equipped with physical facilities needed to these children. Even the teachers working in these schools are also not having proper awareness, attitude and skills to handle these children (Reddy, G.L. 2004). There are occasions that these children are denied admission for enrolment into the schools saying their disabilities will hamper the abilities of normal children. Here and there, there are schools for these disabled children and most of the time the parents of the disabled children are unaware of these schools and are ignorant of the education of their children. The teachers working in the existing special schools are also not well trained with the teaching methodology to be used to compensate the disabilities of the children.

The above mentioned multifaceted problems of education facilitating dropout, wastage and stagnation in Indian educational scenario leaving the concepts like Universalisation of Primary Education and Cent Per cent Literacy at the cross roads. To set right this situation, there is an urgent need for innovative practices such as increasing the infrastructural facilities by linking the community with the school, effective utilisation of existing infrastructural facilities, reducing student-teacher ratio, converting single teacher schools into multiple teacher schools, shift from conventional teaching to innovative methods of teaching to accommodate below average, above average children and children with physical disabilities in the normal classrooms and development of appropriate graded curriculum keeping the mental abilities and disabilities of students in the mind.

Concept, Meaning and Importance of Special Education

In any classroom one can observe students with average, below average and above average mental abilities. The student with average abilities can follow the classroom teacher's instructions and can succeed in oral as well as written examinations. In fact, the classroom teacher is keeping the average student in mind while giving instruction. The below average student is unable to follow the teacher and experience failures in learning by contributing to the concept, stagnation and dropout. For the above average student the classroom teaching is not challenging and motivating. As a result, these students will be the potential disruptive students in the class. In due course they are the potential failures, which in turn leads to wastage, dropout and stagnation. Apart from the above two categories there are children with slow learning, children with speech and language disorders (reading, writing, and spelling disorders) and children with physical and mental disabilities. These children's physical needs, social, psychological, and instructional needs are entirely different from normal (average) children. They need special materials, instructional techniques and facilities to compensate their disabilities or to promote their abilities within the classroom or outside the classrooms of normal schools and special schools.

Special education is nothing but the specially designed instructional programmes, which are applied to exceptional children such as physically handicapped, hearing, impaired, visually impaired and orthopaedically handicapped children), mentally retarded, gifted, slow learners and children with learning difficulties. These instructional programmes are different from the education of normal children but they are equally good to educate normal children. Special Education is defined by Daniel P. Hallahan and James M. Kauffman (1991) as 'specially designed instruction that meets the unusual needs of an exceptional child'.

Daniel P. Hallahan and James M. Kauffman (1991) also defined exceptional children, as 'children are those who require special education and related services if they are to realize their full human potential'. Special materials, teaching techniques or equipment and/or facilities may be required for exceptional children.

Exceptional children are children who have physical, mental, behavioural, or sensory characteristics that differ from the majority of children such that they require special education and related services to develop to their maximum capacity. The category includes children with communication disorders, mental retardation, hearing, visual and orthopaedic disabilities, learning disabilities, behaviour disorders, multiple handicaps, high intelligence and unique talents. Special education is designed to respond to the unique characteristics of the above said children whose needs cannot be met by the standard school curriculum.

Special education is designed to circumvent their deficiency and making them to cope up with the normal peer group as much as possible. Special education may be in various forms such as:

1. Assistance in a regular classroom by the regular classroom teacher;
2. Assistance from the itinerant teacher who moves from school to school to support special needs children;

3. Special self-contained classes is used for small group of special children;
4. Special classroom teaching or in a combination of special classroom and the regular classroom;
5. The another form of special education is organising special schools for children with severe physical and mental disabilities. For e.g. special schools for visually impaired, hearing impaired, mentally retarded, orthopaedically handicapped, schools for gifted/ talented. These children can not get benefit from the normal schools and needs special physical facilities, instructional methods, equipments to compensate their physical and mental disabilities. Likewise, gifted children require challenging tasks in the form of curricular and co-curricular activities and require special facilities and instructional programmes.

A normal classroom generally consists of children who belong to diverse categories such as-below average, average, bright, apart from physically and mentally handicapped, etc. An instructional programme must meet the needs of all these categories. Hence special education is not only meant to enable the exceptional children to surmount their learning problems but it also conducive for normal students in regular classroom.

Whether it is in regular classrooms in normal schools or in special schools, special education is very important for exceptional children. Without special education these children cannot develop independent living skills and social skills. So special education is indispensable for them.

Concept of Mental Retardation

As already stated, mental retardation is one of the major areas of special education. Mentally retarded or handicapped children are characterised by low intelligence in comparison with normal children and there are various degrees of this retardation. Alfred Binet (1905) was assigned this problem by Ministry of Education in France suggested a method for grading mental retardation. Binet, (1908) introduced the concept of

'Mental age' based upon the idea that the majority of the children of a particular age are of normal intelligence and they have a mental level approximating that age, which mental level could be termed as their 'mental age'. If some child falls short in his/her performance of certain tasks, from the performance of the majority of the children of his age, he/she is said to have a lower mental age. For e.g., if a child of eight years had his performance on certain adequately determined tasks equal to that of the majority of the 6 years old then he had the mental age of 6 years. So mentally retarded individuals are those deficient in general intellectual ability that their inability to take care for themselves with disruptive behaviour.

Early history provides an excellent example of how retarded or other handicapped persons were exploited or became victims of cruel practices. For e.g., the Spartan of Greece believed that only the strong should survive, therefore they abandoned anyone who was handicapped (Kanner, 1964). The Romans on the other hand found the retarded to be amusing and many families of the ruling class kept such people in their homes as court jesters a practice that continued into the early history of both France and Germany (Kanner, 1964).

During the late 18th century and into the 19th century, some of the first attempts to educate handicapped persons were made. Jean Marie Itard (1774-1838) a medieval doctor, greatly influenced the field of special education through his work with a wild boy who was found in the woods near Averyon in France. Itard believed that through systematic training Victor's mental deficiency could be eliminated (Kanner, 1964). Thus the field of mental retardation has undergone number of exciting changes.

Once upon a time mentally retarded children are considered as clumsy, drooling and helpless creature. There are various terms used in the past such as amenitia, idiocy, feeble minded, moron, imbecile and oligophrenia. Today, we know this is simply not true. First most children classified as mentally retarded are mildly retarded and look like the hypothetical average child living next door. Second, it can be misleading to characterize even the more severely retarded as helpless. With advanced methods of providing educational and vocational training, we find that retarded people are capable of leading more independent lives than was previously thought not possible. If given appropriate preparation, many are able to live and work with relatively small amounts of help from others.

Definitions of Mental Retardation

Much of the change in the attitude has come from changes in the definition of mental retardation. There are many definitions of mental retardation.

Jane Mercer (1973) holds that it is the individual's social system that determines whether he or she is retarded. She notes that most mentally retarded children particularly those who are higher functioning, do not "Officially" become retarded until they enter school. The school as a social system has certain set of expectations some children do not meet (Daniel P. Hallahan, James M. Kauffman, 1991).

According to Heber (1961) mental deficiency or retardation refers to sub average general intellectual functioning, which originates during the developmental period and is associated with impairments in adaptive behaviour. Sub average here was understood as one standard deviation below the population mean which was to be taken as 100 I.Q. and 1 standard deviation meant 15 to 16 I.Q. points, which meant that people below 85 or 84 I.Q. were to be classified as retarded. The developmental period was regarded from 1st year to 16 years of life. This definition is not acceptable as impairment of adaptive behaviour also could be due to other reasons and not due to retardation.

Tredgold (1970) defined that it is "a state of arrested or incomplete development of mind so severe that the patient is incapable of leading an independent life or of guarding himself against serious exploitation in the case of a child, that he will be so incapable when an adult".

The definition given by American Publication was, mentally retarded individual are said to be those, "who are so deficient in general intellectual ability that their inability to care for themselves, coupled with their disruptive behaviour in some cases, is so severe, when compared with their age-mates in the community, that they require assistance, care and protection in excess of that which average parents can be expected to provide during their childhood or that which average communities should be able to provide during their adulthood."

Then they revised the definition and American view-point is that the mentally retarded be better called as suffering from 'General bearing disabilities' as mental deficiency or retardation implies had stigmatising and the three categories of the retarded as idiots, imbeciles and morons be better called as custodial, trainable and educable. Still less derogatory terms used are severely or profoundly, moderately, and mildly retarded for these categories of the mentally retarded children. There is a fourth category with I.Q. between 75-80 or 90 called border line defective or feebleminded, educationally called as 'slow learner'.

Bijou (1966) and The American Association on Mental Retardation formerly known as American Association on Mental Deficiency also defined mental retardation.

Behavioural Definition

The articulation of the behavioural definition is generally attributed to Bijou (1966) who stated, "a retarded individual is one who has a limited repertory of behaviour shaped by events that constitute his history. In this definition Bijou emphasizes observable behaviour and pays little or no attention to non-observable internal mental processes.

The behavioural definition of mental retardation quite often presents problems to special educators who have not been trained in applied behavioural analysis. Neisworth and Smith (1978) point out that a major shortcoming is its failure to quantify. What is meant by a limited behavioural repertoire? In other words, the definition does not describe the point at which the limitations in a person's repertoire behaviours indicate he or she is retarded. Macmillan and Foreness (1973) point out that this model does not take in account some of the more widely accepted concepts regarding human growth and development that were pioneered by Piaget and other developmental psychologists.

American Association on Mental Deficiency Definition (1983)

Mental retardation is recognized by all major classification systems. The definition offered by the American Association on Mental Deficiency which has led efforts to understand and ameliorate mental retardation founded in 1876, which is later, named as American Association on mental retardation. This organization has long provided definitions of mental retardation that have been adopted by others, including the DSM (Diagnostic and Statistical Manual of Mental Disorders).

The American Association on Mental Deficiency (Grossman, 1983) defines "Mental retardation as a significantly sub average general intellectual functioning, resulting in or associated with concurrent impairments in adaptive behaviour and manifested during the developmental period."

'General Intellectual functioning' is defined as the results obtained by the administration of standardized general intelligence tests developed for the purpose, and adapted to the conditions of the region/country.

'Significantly sub average' is defined as I.Q. of 70 or below on standardized measures of intelligence. The upper limit is intended as a guideline, it could be extended to 75 or more depending upon the reliability of intelligence test used.

'Adaptive behaviour' is defined as the degree with which the individual meets the standards of personal independence and social responsibility expected of his age and cultural group. The expectations of adaptive behaviour vary with the chronological age. The deficits in adaptive behaviour may be reflected in the following areas:

During infancy and early childhood in 7 yrs.

(a) Sensory and motor skill development;

(b) Communication skills (including speech and language);

(c) Self-help skills;

(d) Socialization;

During childhood and adolescence in 18 yrs.

(e) Application of basic academic skills to daily life activities;

(f) Application of appropriate reasoning and judgement in the mastery of the environment;

(g) Social Skills;

During late adolescence and adult life in above 18 yrs.

(h) Vocational and social responsibilities and performance.

'Developmental period' is defined as the period of time between conception and 18th birthday.

American Association on Mental Retardation Paradigm Shift in Definition

In its latest publication manual 'Mental Retardation: Definition, Classification, and Systems of Support', AAMR modified its definition of mental retardation, claiming a paradigm shift.

The following is the definition currently offered by AAMR (1992).

Mental retardation refers to substantial limitations in present functioning. It is characterized by significantly sub average intellectual functioning, existing concurrently with related limitations in two or more of the following applicable adaptive skill areas: Communication, self-care, home living, social skills, community use, self-direction, health and safety, functional academics, leisure and work. Mental retardation manifests before age 18 (Luckasson et al. 1992, p.5).

The current definition of mental retardation reflects the long history of how the condition has been conceptualized and identified. AAMR claim a "Paradigm Shift" in its definition because the shift has to do with a stronger rejection of mental retardation as an absolute trait of the individual and a greater emphasis on environmental interactions that influence how the person is functioning.

The AAMR's model of mental retardation figure-1, shows how mental retardation is conceptualized and individual is viewed as functioning in complex ways in a socio-cultural context.

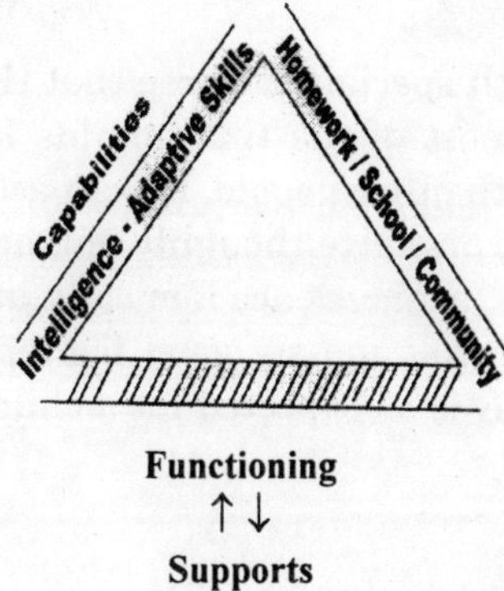

Functioning

↑↓

Supports

AAMR'S model of Mental Retardation (Luckasson et al., 1992).

Adaptive Behaviour

In 1959, AAMR first included deficits in adaptive functioning as a criterion for mental retardation. Subsequently AAMR offered the following definition:

Adaptive behaviour refers to the quality of everyday performance in coping with environmental demands. The quality of adaptation is mediated by level of intelligence; thus, the two concepts overlap in meaning. It is evident, however, from consideration of the definition of adaptive behaviour, with its stress on everyday. Coping, that adaptive behaviour refers to what people do to take care of them and to relate to others in daily living rather than the abstract potential implied by intelligence (Grossman, 1983, p.42).

Mental retardation is different from mental illness. Mental retardation is the deficiency in intellectual functioning of an individual and it is uncurable and permanent phenomena. Whereas, mental illness refers to the temporary or permanent mental deviation from normal behaviour. It can be curable and most of the times temporary in nature.

Mental Health

Good mental health implies freedom from mental illness, happiness and a wholesome development of character and personality.

Mental health specialists agree that the mentally healthy child is happy most of the time, builds lasting and positive relationships with other people, has an accurate perception of reality, is able to organize thoughts and actions to accomplish reasonable goals, achieves academically at a level close to his or her potential, has mostly good feelings about himself or herself and behaves as expected for a child of a given age and sex.

Mental Illness

Mental illness is revealed by opposite characteristics—unhappiness, trouble in getting along with others, disorganisation, underachievement, feelings of worthlessness and inadequacy and in appropriate behaviour.

Classification of Mental Retardation

AAMR's new model eliminates classifying people by IQ levels and instead classifies by needed environmental supports. But in early days, mental retardation was classified by different methods. They are: medical, psychological and educational classification. The medical classification is based on the causes. The psychological classification based on the level of intelligence and the educational classification on the current level of functioning of the mentally retarded person/child.

Medical Classification

1. Infections and intoxications
2. Trauma or physical agent
3. Metabolism or Nutrition
4. Gross brain disease. (Post natal)
5. Unknown prenatal influences
6. Chromosomal abnormality

7. Gestational disorder
8. Psychiatric disorder
9. Environmental influence
10. Other influences

Psychological Classification based on IQ

1. Mildly retarded — 50-70
2. Moderately retarded — 35-49
3. Severely retarded — 20-34
4. Profoundly retarded — Below 20

Educational Classification

1. Educable
2. Trainable
3. Custodial

The various classifications provide an understanding of the level at which the mentally retarded person functions with respect to his education, appropriate behaviour and the degree of his independence.

AAMR Systems Classification

AAMR Systems Classification is given in Table—1.1.

Table—1.1 Level of retardation indicated by IQ range obtained on Measure of General Intellectual functioning.

Term	*IQ range for level*
Mild mental retardation	50-55 to app 70
Moderate mental retardation	35-40 to 50-55
Severe mental retardation	20-25 to 35-40
Profound mental retardation	Below 20-25

Source: H.J.Grossman, (1983) (Ed.), Classification in Mental Retardation (Washington, DC: American Association on Mental Deficiency, p.13).

There are three reasons why most professionals agree that the AAMR system is most useful.

1. The terms used—mild, moderate, severe and profound retardation-do not carry the degree of negative stereotypying of earlier descriptions ("idiot, feeble minded"). They are adjectives commonly applied to a vast array of other things or conditions besides retardation.
2. The terms used emphasize the level of functioning of the individual
3. The use of bands of IQ scores for 50-55 as the cut off between mild and moderate retardation leaves some room for clinical judgement and recognises that IQ scores are not perfect predictors of a person's level of retardation. As per AAMR manual someone whose Weschler IQ is 53 might be diagnosed as either mild or moderate depending upon other factors such as relative difference in performance and verbal IQ or results of other tests (Grossman, 1983, p.13).

As per Educator's classification, Educable mentally retarded (EMR) individuals are those with IQs between 75 or 70 (more and more school systems are now using 70 whereas previously they used 75 and 50). Trainable mentally retarded (TMR) persons have IQs between 50 and 25. Since the passage of PL 94-142, schools have been obligated to serve children with IQs below 25 and these individuals are commonly referred to as severely and profoundly handicapped (SPH). In general, persons classified as EMR can learn some basic academic subjects. The curriculum for individuals classified TMR, on the other hand, concentrates more on functional academic subjects with emphasis on self-help and vocational skills.

One disadvantage of this system is that some educators have at times take the categories too literally. Some children labelled as TMR were denied children to learn some academic subject matter within their intellectual reach. Likewise, students classified as EMR need to learn self help and vocational skills. Intelligence test scores are not reliable and valid enough in determining the different educational objectives for one child with IQ of 51 classified as educable and the other with an IQ of 49 classified as trainable.

New Classification by AAMR (1992)

AAMR's new model eliminates classifying people by IQ levels and instead classifies by needed environmental supports. For each person descriptions are to be given of strengths and weaknesses with regard to four aspects:

(a) Intellectual functioning and adaptive skills;

(b) Psychological and emotional functioning;

(c) Physical functioning and health;

(d) The person's current environment and the environment that would be optimal for continued growth.

Then a profile is developed of needed supports across the four aspects. The profile stipulates, for each aspect, a level of support required: intermittent, limited, extensive or pervasive. Thus instead of a broad diagnosis based on IQ such as "severe mental retardation" the diagnose is might be "a person with mental retardation with extensive supports needed in the areas of social skills and self direction" (Luckasson et al. 1992, p. 34). This approach recognizes that needs for support might be different in one area of functioning from another.

AAMR's concept of mental retardation as dynamically linked to the environment rather than being viewed as a static quality of the individual. Table—1.2 defines the Levels of Needed Support:

Table—1.2 AAMR's Levels of Needed Support

Intermittent:	Support on "as needed" basis. Person needs sporadic supports or short-term supports during life-span transition or crises (e.g. during job loss or acute medical crisis). Supports may be high or low intensity.
Limited:	High or low intensity supports are needed consistently for only a limited time (e.g., time-limited, employment training).
Extensive:	Supports characterized by regular involvement (e.g., daily), in atleast some environments (e.g., work or home) and are not time-limited (e.g., long-term home living supports).
Pervasive:	Supports characterized by constancy and high intensity across environments. Potentially life sustaining in nature. Typically involve more staff members and intrusiveness.

DSM (Diagnostic and Statistical Manual of Mental disorders) Classification

DSM-IV is now at odds with AAMR's new classification by needed environmental support and it continues to classify mental retardation by intelligence levels. Table—1.3 shows the four levels employed by DSM-IV and a general description of functioning for each level. Comparable classification used by educators in the United States is also indicated which consists of 3 subgroups based on expectations for learning: educable, trainable and severely/profoundly handicapped. This classification is relevant to guide the management of intellectually handicapped students for many years and is still sometimes employed.

Table—1.3 Levels of Mental Retardation According to DSM IV

	Level	*IQ Range*	*Per cent of MR Population*	*Functioning*
1.	Mild (Educable)	50-55 to about 70	85	1. Social and communication skills usually develop in pre-school years. 2. Have minimal sensorimotor deficits. 3. Can acquire about sixth grade academic skills by late teens. 4. Usually achieve about vocational and social skills for self-support 5. May need guidance, assistance and supervised living. But often live successfully in the community.
2.	Moderate (Trainable)	35-40 to 50-55	10	1. Communication skills usually develop in early childhood. 2. Attend to personal care, with support.

(Contd...)

Level	IQ Range	Per cent of MR Population	Functioning
			3. Are unlikely to progress beyond second-grade academic skills. 4. Can benefit from social and occupation skills training and do supervised unskilled or semi skilled work. 5. Adapt well to supervised community living.
3. Severe (Severely or profoundly handicapped)	20-25 to 35-40	3-4	1. May learn to talk and minimally care for self at school age. 2. Have limited ability to profit from preacademic training. 3. In adulthood, may perform simple tasks with supervision. 4. In most cases, adapt well to community living with family or in group homes.
4. Profound (severely or profoundly handicapped)	Below 20-25	1-2	1. In most cases, have a neurological condition. Have sensorimotor impairments in childhood with training, may show improvement in motor, self-care and communication skills. 2. May do simple supervised tasks. 3. For optimal development, require structure, constant supervision with individual caretaker.

Source: Based on APA 1994; and Singh, Oswald and Ellis, 1998

Thus a distinction is commonly made between mild retardation and more severe retardation with the IQ of about 50 marking the boundary. AAMR's paradigm shift can be beneficial in that it encourages the view that human functioning at any level of intelligence is influenced by an individual's interactions with the environment.

Prevalence of Mental Retardation

The prevalence of mental retardation is estimated at about 2 to 3 per cent of the general population when IQ is taken as the criterion as it often is (Singh, Oswald, & Ellis, 1998). When Mental Retardation defined by both IQ and adaptive behaviour, as recommended, prevalence drops to under 1 per cent (Scott, 1994). This difference might reflect the fact that about half of those with mental retardation are not identified because their behaviour is sufficiently adaptive in their environments. Prevalence data are especially interesting when age and severity of retardation are inspected. Pre-school youngsters are only rarely identified and most have IQs below 15, apparently because the more severe cases are obvious and therefore elicit attention. But a dramatic shift occurs when children enter school. Prevalence increases as more mild retardation is identified, probably because the children are unable to meet the new demands in this situation.

It is generally considered that 2 per cent of the population constitute persons with mental retardation. However, there is no systematic National Survey conducted to determine the prevalence of mental retardation in India. Recently, it has been estimated that in India, there are about 20 million persons who are mildly retarded and about 4 million persons who are moderately and severely retarded. Table—1.4 gives the details of various prevalence studies conducted in India till 1983. It can be observed from the table that the figures for prevalence of mental retardation in India vary from 0.22 to 32.7 per thousand populations. This is because the methodology, the time, the type of population and the sample size were not uniform in all the studies and the operational definition of a case of mental retardation varied from one study to the other.

In addition, these surveys were carried out with the intention of finding out the psychiatric morbidity and mental retardation.

Table—1.4 Prevalence of Mental Retardation in India

Sl. No.	*Investigators*	*Year*	*Place*	*Population studied*	*Type of community*	*Prevalence per 1000 Population*
1.	Surya et al.	1964	Pondicherry	2,731	Urban, Slum	0.7
2.	Sethi et al.	1967	Locknow	1,733	Urban	22.5
3.	Gopinath	1968	Bangalore	423	Rural	4.72
4.	Dube	1970	Agra	29,468	Mixed	3.7
5.	Elnagar	1971	Hooghly	1,383	Rural	1.4
6.	Sethi et al.	1972	Lucknow	2,691	Rural	25.3
7.	Varghese	1973	Vellore	2,904	Urban	3.2
8.	Sethi et al.	1974	Lucknow	4,481	Urban	10.5
9.	Thacore et al.	1975	Lucknow	2,696	Urban	14.0
10.	Nandi	1976	Calcutta	1,060	Rural	2.8
11.	Nandi	1976	Calcutta	1,078	Rural	3.7
12.	Carstairs and Kapur	1980	Kota	9,111	Rural	10.0
13.	Nandi	1980	Calcutta	4,053	Rural	8.6
14.	Nandi	1980	Calcutta	1,864	Mixed	10.7
15.	Shah	1980	Ahmedabad	2,712	Urban	1.8
16.	Isaac and Kapur	1982	Bangalore	4,209	Rural	3.6
17.	Shalini	1983	Bangalore	451	Rural	32.7
18.	ICMR	1983	Bangalore	35,548	Rural	1.32
19.	ICMR	1983	Baroda	39.655	Rural	2.33
20.	ICMR	1983	Calcutta	34,582	Rural	0.58
21.	ICMR	1983	Patiala	36,595	Rural	0.22

Source: Mental Retardation : A Manual for Psychologists, NIMH, 1989.

Summary

Education makes an individual not to remain as a parasite on society. Realising this, the Government of India has introduced education as a fundamental right to every citizen.

To provide this fundamental right, so many programmes have been launched without any caste, creed, religion and community discrimination. In spite of these programmes, the concepts like Universalisation of Primary Education and Cent Per cent Literacy are at the crossroads. The reason being the high rate of dropout, wastage and stagnation particularly among the children coming from the deprived sections of communities such as SC & ST. Wastage and stagnation is also high in rural and urban slums. High student-teacher ratio, single teacher schools, handling multiple classes and subjects by a single teacher accounts for wastage and stagnation. Certain groups such as pupil with physical disabilities and mental disabilities are left without proper attention in normal schools. The schools are also not well equipped with the physical facilities and the teaching methodologies to be used for these children. Teachers working in special schools are also not well trained to handle these disabled children. The above mentioned multifaceted problems facilitate the dropout, wastage and stagnation in India sub continent. To set right this problem there is a need to have a specialized instructional procedures, materials and/or facilities to teach disabled children which is termed as special education. Special Education means 'specially designed instruction that meets the unusual needs of an exceptional child'. Special Education may be of various forms such as—assistance in the regular classroom by regular classroom teacher, support by itinerant teacher who moves from school to school, special care in the self-contained classes to certain groups of students, extra support given in special classroom or in combination of both special classroom and regular classroom, and organising special schools which are more suitable for children with severe physical and mental abilities.

Mentally retarded or handicapped, are characterised by low intelligence in comparison with normal children. Early history provides an excellent example of how retarded or other handicapped were exploited or became victims of cruel practices. Mentally retarded children are considered as clumsy, drooling and helpless creatures during olden days. Today we know this is simply not true. Much of the change in the attitude has come from changes in the definition of mental retardation.

Classification of mental retardation also has a long history and it had a paradigm shift by various educationists, psychologists, and psychiatrists. Among the various classifications of mental retardation, most of the professionals classify according to the severity of the retardation. AAMR classifies mental retardation based on IQ as mild mental retardation (IQ 50-55 to 70), moderate mental retardation (IQ 35-40 to 50-55), severe mental retardation (IQ 20-25 to 35-40) and profound mental retardation (IQ below 20-25). Prevalence of mental retardation is estimated at about 2 to 3 per cent of the general population when IQ is taken as the criterion as it often is. However, there is no systematic National Survey conduced to determine the prevalence of mental retardation in India. Prevalence of mental retardation in India varies from 0.22 to 32.7 per thousand populations based on the existing surveys in India.

2

Factors, Causes and Characteristics Associated with Mental Retardation

OBJECTIVES

This chapter clearly deals with the factors resulting mental retardation, causes and preventive measures for mental retardation. It also pinpoints the other associated conditions/ problems of mental retardation and also the various characteristics of mental retardation. After reading this chapter one can understand

1. Factors resulting mental retardation
2. Causes for mental retardation
3. Preventive measures of mental retardation
4. Associated problems of mental retardation
5. Characteristics of mental retardation

Introduction

Mental retardation is the result of so many factors. An analysis of such factors, causes and characteristics of mental retardation, preventive measures and associated problems in mental retardation are discussed in this chapter for better conceptual clarity and understanding.

Factors Resulting Mental Retardation

Although mental retardation is associated with hundreds of specific medical and genetic conditions as well as with psycho-social disadvantage, causation is not clearly identified in an estimated 20 to 30 per cent of cases of severe mental retardation and in 50 to 60 per cent of mild mental retardation (Gillberg 1997, Luckasson et al. 1992).

Historically causes for mental retardation are categorized into biological and psycho-social factors (Luckasson et al. 1992). Scott (1994) recognized three kinds of influences that have been widely discussed: Organic risk factors, polygenic inheritance and psycho-social/cultural influences

Organic Risk Factors

Organic risk factor attributes to mental retardation. Organic risk factor implies that biological conditions account for disordered brain function and intellectual deficiency. Major pathological causes are known and believed to be primary in about 25 per cent of mental retardation cases (Scott and Carran, 1987). Organic problems are associated with all levels of mental retardation but especially with more severe retardation. Known pathology exists in an estimated 55 to 75 per cent of children with severe retardation but in only 10 to 25 per cent with mild retardation (Scott, 1994).

Genetic Abnormalities

A variety of genetic aberrations both inherited and non-inherited, are associated with specific syndromes of mental retardation. A few genetic syndromes account for a relatively large number of cases of mental retardation. Three syndromes—Down syndrome, Fragile × Syndrome and Williams Syndrome demonstrate different genetic abnormalities and distinct clinical features.

Down Syndrome

Down Syndrome aberrations in the number and structure of chromosomes are the single most common cause of severe retardation (Simonoff et al. 1996). Children with Down syndrome are born with a variety of physical abnormalities that results in a common resemblance. Epicanthal folds at the corners of the ears and the upward slant of the eyes, which gave rise to the name “mongolism”. Other features include facial flatness, fissured and thick tongues, broad hands and feet, and poor muscle tone (Aman, Hammer, and Rojahn, 1993).

Intelligence ranges in the moderate to profound levels of retardation and is occasionally higher developmental deficits during early life and amidst many spurts and regressions (Szymanski and Kaplan 1991); the rate of development progressively slow throughout childhood and adolescence (Bregman and Hodapp, 1991; Carr, 1994). Language functioning is typically delayed and relatively weak, weakness in scanning and extract information from the environment (Laws, 1998; Rossen et al. 1996). Social skills are relatively high as these children generally cooperate with others and respect social rules. At the same time, their emotional development is slowed and the emotions seem muted (Whitman, O’ Callaghan and Sommer, 1997).

Fragile X Syndrome

This condition is one of many specific syndromes associated with mental retardation that are inherited in Mendelian single-gene patterns. It is second to Down syndrome as a cause of retardation affecting about 5 per cent cases of more severe retardation and 5 per cent cases of mild retardation (Gillberg 1997). There is a notable and predictable decline in IQ from about ten to fifteen years of age (State, King, and Dykens, 1997). They are relative weaknesses in short term memory, visual motor coordination, sequential processing, mathematics and attention. They display relative strength in adaptive behaviour. Behaviour difficulties include hyperactivity, stereotypic, and poor peer relations.

Females with Fragile × Syndrome display mental retardation and when they do, it tends to be mild although similar to the male profile. Learning disabilities are common in females with one affected x chromosomes, as well as various behaviour problems and social impairments.

Williams Syndrome

This syndrome is a rare disorder associated with a gene deletion on chromosome 7 (State et al. 1997). Characteristics are distinctive "elfinlike" face, growth deficiency, cardiac and kidney problems, and abnormal calcium metabolism. The syndrome is typically associated with mild to moderate retardation with the mean IQ being in the middle fifties (Howlin, Daves and Udwin 1998). Deficiencies exist in abilities such as general knowledge, abstract conceptualisation, and problem solving (Rossen et al. 1996). Performance IQ tends to be significantly lower than verbal IQ, visual spatial skills are below what would be expected in keeping with the children's mental age. Deficits appear distinct and are striking (Rossen et al. 1996). At adolescent stage there is an inability to perceive gross differences in spatial orientation and to copy simple stick figures. Selective attention is given to details rather than to whole configurations.

Prenatal and Perinatal Factors

Organic risk factors associated with prenatal development and/or perinatal events are commonly encountered in cases of mental retardation (Gillberg, 1997).

Prenatal exposure to disease, chemicals, drugs, radiation, poor nutrition and Rh incompatibility may jeopardize the intellectual development of the child. Low birth weight and prematurity are also associated with neurological and intellectual deficits (Bregman and Hodapp, 1991).

Complications occurring at birth, such as head injury, seizures, and anoxia, can also take a toll. Anoxia occurs in about five out of one thousand births, about 20 per cent of the infants are adversely affected, and cerebral palsy with mental retardation can follow (Scott 1994).

Postnatal Factors

Mental retardation may also be caused postnatally by a variety of variables, such as seizures, brain tumours, infectious diseases such as encephalitis and meningitis, child playing with lead and mercury coated toys, head injuries from auto bicycle and other accidents. All these factors can interfere with nervous system functioning and development. Many post natal circumstances undoubtedly put the child or adolescent at organic risk and can also cause retardation as complications arising from childhood diseases such as whooping cough, chicken pox, and measles.

Polygenic Inheritance Influences/Factors

Polygenic influences derive from multiple genes whose effects combine to produce variation in intelligence in normal population. Current understanding of hereditary influence on tested intelligence has a firm base in behaviour genetic research. Intelligence test performance of identical twins is overall more similar than that of fraternal twins (McGue et al. 1993). This findings holds even on specific intellectual tasks. When identical twins are reared apart, similarity decreases but is still high. Studies of families and adopted children lend support to the twin findings. In general, it is estimated that about 50 per cent of the variation in tested intelligence in populations is due to genetic transmission of multiple genes (Plomin, De Fries and McClearn, 1990). Most of this research has been conducted with non-retarded persons. Few studies with retarded individuals similarly implicate polygenic inheritance (Thompson, 1997).

Research studies also suggest that polygenic influences vary with the level of retardation. There are evidences that pathological organic factors are more strongly associated with the more severe levels of retardation. The opposite appears to hold for polygenic influences. One family study revealed that the IQs of siblings of children with severe retardation averaged 103 hinting that severe retardation did not "Run" in families and that some specific organic factor caused retardation in the affected child. In contrast, the IQs of siblings of children with mild retardation averaged 85, suggesting general family influence, perhaps polygenic inheritance, psycho-social effects, or a combination of these (Broman et al., 1987; Scott, 1994).

Psycho-social/Cultural Factors

It is reasonable to assume that malnutrition, inadequate medical and prenatal care, disease-proned conditions and other health hazards associated with poverty all contribute to lowered intellectual functioning. In addition, it appears that a number of other less readily observable factors help to produce mental retardation. These are related to child rearing practices, the home environment, family structure and similar factors. Causative factors of these types are known as "psycho-social factors".

Mild retardation caused by psycho-social factors is almost always difficult to identify in young children. Most of these children are not identified until they reach school age, when it is discovered that they have difficulty with educational tasks.

The American Association on Mental Deficiency (Grossman, 1983) uses four criteria to determine whether a child's retardation can be attributed to psycho-social disadvantages.

1. Intelligence and adaptive behaviour are at retarded levels of functioning
2. There is retarded intellectual functioning in the immediate family and usually the larger family circle as well.
3. There is no clear evidence of brain damage in the child.
4. In most instances, the home environment is impoverished.

Pioneers in mental retardation do not believe that intelligence and other characteristics of the personality are caused exclusively by either genetic or environmental factors. The current belief is that these traits result from the interaction of genetic and environmental variables. It is believed that intelligence can be limited to a certain range by genetic factors but within that range the environment will determine an individual's intelligence. This means that children who have the genetic potential to be only mildly retarded may have a much lower level of intelligence if they are raised in a very poor environment. So, it is important that children be raised in as rich and stimulating environment as possible. In Table—2.1, the metabolic disorders associated with mental retardation are presented.

Table—2.1 Metabolic Disorders Associated with Mental Retardation

	Disorder and Mechanism	*Metabolic Disturbance*	*Manifestation*	*Treatment*
1.	Phenylketon uria recessive inheritance	Inability to convert the amino acid phenylalanine due to deficient liver enzyme.	Retardation, hyperactivity, unpredictable behaviour convulsions, eczema can occur.	Diet low in phenylalanine, if begun early, can prevent or reduce retardation.
2.	Maple syrup urine disease. Recessive inheritance	Abnormal metabolism of amino acids—leucine, isoleucone, valine	Infants develop rigidity, seizures, respiratory, irregularities, hypoglycemia. Most die in few months if untreated or are severely retarded.	Diet low in leucine, isoleucine, valine is used.
3.	Schilder's disease Sex-linked inheritance	Decrease of fats in (NS resulting in demyelination of cerebral white matter)	Onset more common in older children and adults. Personality and behavioural changes. Paresis, cortical blindness and deafness, convulsions, dementia	No established treatment; may respond to steroids.
4.	Galactosemia recessive inheritance	Inability to convert galactose (carbohydrate to glucose)	After a few days of milk intake, jaundice, vomiting, diarrhoea, failure to thrive. Leads to rapid death or mental retardation.	Early galactose-free-diet permits normality.

Causes of Mental Retardation

Causes for mental retardation can be categorized into three stages. They are:

1. Prenatal Causes
2. Perinatal Causes
3. Postnatal Causes

(a) Prenatal Causes

1. *Genetic and Chromosomal Disorder:* Genes are the basic units of heredity. They control and direct the process of growth and development that occur in each of our cells. A defective gene can interrupt the biochemical process that occurs in the cells, which in turn affect certain physical and mental characteristics. Defect in the genes, transmitted from the parent to the off spring can result in certain conditions with mental retardation. Whether the parents may have the defect or not, they may not manifest the condition. Some genetic disorders result metabolic abnormality and a specific enzyme may be deficient or absent. This results in accomplishes of specific substance in the body including the brain resulting in brain damage. This causes mental retardation. Phenylketonuria, mucopoly saccharidosis, lipidoses etc., are some of the genetic disorders.

There are 23 pairs of chromosomes in each human cell. Every person gets half the number of chromosomes from each parent. Errors in chromosomes produce conditions with medical problems and most of these conditions cause mental retardation. The error may be in the structure of the chromosome or in the number of chromosomes being too many or too few.

1. Down Syndrome
2. Fragile ×-Syndrome
3. William's Syndrome

2. Infections during the first three months of pregnancy can damage the developing brain of the foetus. If the mother is suffering with cytomegalic inclusion disease, toxoplasmosis, syphilis and tuberculosis there is every possibility that the foetus brain development will be affected.

3. Maternal diseases such as diabetes mellitus and high blood pressure, chronic kidney problems and malnutrition in the mother can damage the growing foetus.

4. Hypothyroidism (lack of thyroid hormone) in mother during pregnancy may lead on to the birth of a child with cretinism (a disorder of the endocrine characterized by lack of thyroid hormone. It is due to the diet that is deficit in iodine). Hyperthyroidism which is the condition of excess thyroid hormone in the mother can produce defects in the central nervous system of the growing foetus leading to mental retardation.

5. Exposure to x-ray in the early months of pregnancy may lead to microcephaly. Microcephaly is one of the several cranial disorders that can be caused by genetic defects or by non-genetic factors such as exposure of the mother to excessive dosage of x-rays during pregnancy. It can be caused by infections such as rubella or AIDS (Rubinsten 1989).

6. Congenital defects of the central nervous system such as hydrocephalous (children are short and have small skull) and a number of defects of the brain and spinal cord are associated with mental retardation.

7. Rh incompatibility may affect the intellectual development of the child. A woman with Rh negative blood who is impregnated by an Rh positive male has a chance of producing a foetus with Rh positive blood. When this occurs, the mother's body produces antibodies that attack the foetus as they would attack the foreign substance that has entered the body. Rh

incompatibility rarely affects a first born child. A vaccine called Rho Gam has been developed to prevent Rh factor problems in later pregnancy.

8. Usage of drugs, alcohol and smoking habits during pregnancy will also seriously affect the intellectual development of the child resulting in mental retardation.
9. Infections that may lead to mental retardation can occur in the mother to be or the infant after birth. Rubella (German measles) and herpes simples in the mother can cause retardation in the foetus. Rubella is dangerous during the first three months of pregnancy. The venereal diseases, and herpes simples present a greater risk at later stages of foetal development (Hetherington and Parke, 1986). They may cause brain damage which inturn result in mental retardation.
10. Toxic agents such as cocaine and heroin are more subtle potential "poisons". Consumption of tobacco, caffeine, and even food additives are also having harmful effects resulting in mental retardation.
11. Improper nutrition also causes mental retardation. When the expectant mother is malnourished or when the child once born does not have a proper diet, retardation occurs.
12. Teenage pregnancy may be another cause for mental retardation. Early marriage practices will lead to teenage pregnancy and it may affect foetus brain growth and as a result it leads to mental retardation.

(b) Perinatal Causes

Perinatal events are commonly encountered in cases of mental retardation (Gillberg, 1997).

1. Low birth weight baby (say less than 2kg) is more prone to suffer from delayed mental development and this may lead to mental retardation.
2. Premature birth (Baby born between 24 weeks and 34 week) also accounts for the causes of mental retardation.

3. Lack of oxygen (anoxia) immediately after birth is one of the causes of mental retardation. Anoxia occurs in about five of one thousand births, about 20 per cent of the infants are adversely affected and cerebral palsy with mental retardation can follow (Scott, 1994).
4. Excessive coiling of the umbilical cord around the neck of the newborn can also be the cause of mental retardation.
5. Hard usage of forceps and instruments during delivery may lead to mental retardation.
6. Trauma to the head of the newborn when the position of the baby is complicated during labour.
7. Prolonged labour is also one of the perinatal causes of mental retardation.
8. Toxemia of pregnancy with high blood pressure and fits in the mother also accounts for perinatal causes of mental retardation.
9. Haemorrhage or bleeding in the brain of the newborn may also lead to mental retardation.
10. Severe Jaundice in the newborn due to various causes may also lead to mental retardation.
11. Anaesthetics and painkillers administered to the mother during delivery may also be one of the causes for mental retardation.
12. Abnormal position of the foetus in the uterus is also one of the causes for mental retardation. Birth complications may contribute relatively little to the etiology of mental retardation.

(c) Postnatal Causes

Mental retardation may also be caused postnatally by a variety of variables

1. Malnutrition during postnatal period may affect the nervous system functioning and development. This may result in mental retardation.

2. Head injuries due to blow to the head or by accidents also interfere the nervous system functioning and causes mental retardation.
3. Encephalitis, which is an inflammation of the brain, affects intelligence more severely and results in mental retardation.
4. Paediatric AIDS is also the fastest growing infections causing mental retardation and brain damage (Diamond and Cohen 1987).
5. Childhood diseases like whooping cough, chicken pox and German measles also affect the nervous system resulting in mental retardation.
6. Lead/Mercury poisoning is one of the most important causes of mental retardation. Without proper awareness parents may get the toys coated with lead or mercury. When the child is playing with those toys the lead or mercury will get into the mouth and affects the nervous system functioning and inturn, results mental retardation.
7. Seizures, brain tumors also cause mental retardation.
8. Meningitis, which is an infection of the covering of the brain, may be caused by variety of bacterial or viral agents and it may be one of the causes for mental retardation.
9. PKU (Phenylketonuria) involves the inability of the body to convert a common dietary substance phenylalanine to tyrosine. Accumulation of phenylalanine results in abnormal brain development. Babies should undergo a screening test for PKU in the first few days after birth. Unless a baby with PKU starts a special diet controlling the intake of phenylalanine in infancy and continuous it into middle childhood, the child will develop severe retardation.
10. *Tay-Sachs Disease:* Like PKU Tay-sachs disease can appears when both mother and father are carriers and it results in progressive brain damage and eventual death. The disease can be detected in utero.

Preventive Measures of Mental Retardation

A close look at the factors resulting in mental retardation and causes of mental retardation clearly reveals the need for multidisciplinary approach involving persons from health, welfare and education. Some of the ways and means of preventing mental retardation among children are:

Prenatal Stage

(a) *Genetic Counselling:* Mental retardation can be reduced through genetic counselling. The genetic counsellor regarding the type of disorder, mode of inheritance, risks of recurrence and options available as alternatives can advise persons with potential genetic defects. Pregnant women with a history of genetic problem should be sent to a place where tests to detect such abnormalities in the foetus are available.

(b) Conducting tests like amniocentesis, sonography, chronic villus sampling. Amniocentesis and chronic villus sampling tests are carried out to detect the chromosomal abnormalities. Genetic screening programmes will also help to identify the carriers of defects. In sonography, high frequency sound waves or ultra-sound are converted into a visual picture of the foetus. This technique can be used to detect some major physical malformations such as spina bifida.

(c) Periodic medical check-up for the pregnant woman is very important. If she had deformities in previous deliveries or of repeated abortions she has to be admitted to a hospital for further investigation with good facilities. Drugs without medical prescription should be avoided.

(d) Pregnant women should not be exposed to radiations such as x-rays during early stages of pregnancy.

(e) Immunization should be carried out against diseases such as German measles and tetanus.

(f) Continuous care should be given to the pregnant women who have high blood pressure or repeated fits.

(g) Accident-prone activity such as walking on slippery grounds, climbing on narrow stools and chairs and carrying heavy loads should be avoided during pregnancy.

(h) Consumption of alcohol, tobacco, heroin, and caffeine, cocainine by the mother during pregnancy should be prohibited.

(i) Smoking habit by the mother during pregnancy should also be prohibited.

Perinatal Stage

Brain damage during delivery results, in mental retardation. Difficulties during the time of delivery (prolonged labour; ceasarian delivery etc) is one of the most common causes of mental retardation in developing countries like India since specialized attention is not always available. Proper care during delivery can help in preventing mental retardation.

(a) The qualified personnel should conduct delivery. Complications must be detected early and the impending conditions should be informed to a qualified doctor and abnormal positioning of the foetus in the uterus during delivery should be given due attention by the qualified doctor.

(b) In the case of anoxia (baby is blue when born or if the birth cry is delayed) the baby must be given oxygen immediately and care must be taken to ensure that the baby breathes properly.

(c) If any congenital abnormality is noted the child should be sent to a specialist for management.

Postnatal Stage

(a) A child should be immunized against all infectious diseases such as diphtheria, polio, tetanus, measles, tuberculosis, and whooping cough.

(b) If a child gets fits, drugs must be given to control them and further fits.

(c) In case of epidemics especially those of brain fever (encephalitis) the baby should be given adequate care and see that food and water are not contaminated.

(d) Adequate nutritious food should be given to the child because malnutrition during the developmental period is said to impair brain growth.

(e) Child with small/big head or stiff limbs should be taken to a doctor to prevent further disabilities.

(f) If a child has a high fever the temperature should be brought down immediately by cold sponging and antipyretics.

(g) Gross delay in attaining the proper milestones during the first six months by the child should be tested by an expert for a thorough evaluation of developmental disabilities.

Strategies to Overcome Mental Retardation

Eventhough measures for preventing mental retardation is known to certain extent in the elite communities, the communities like SC, ST and downtrodden are in darkness about the different aspects of mental retardation. It is a well-known fact that awareness and attitudinal change leads to better performance and practices. As India is having vast majority of illiterate and semi literate population, generating proper awareness and development of positive altitudes on the different aspects of mental retardation normally leads for better practices to prevent mental retardation in children. Infact, the field of mental retardation is multidisciplinary in nature where health personnel, educationists and social workers play a dominant role. In this context, it is more sensitive to keep in mind the kind of personnel involved in the programmes, the type of media exploited in different situations and the mode of presentation of material or concepts to the public while developing strategies to sensitise the people for better awareness, development of positive attitudes and healthy practices.

A close look at the educational structure health and welfare facilities available in India will definitely give an idea about the ways and means of exploiting the educational systems and facilities to prevent mental retardation. Integration of educational systems, health and social services definitely play a predominant role for effective prevention of mental retardation. To achieve Cent Per cent Literacy and Universalisation of Primary Education a variety of programmes like formal, non-formal and in formal have been started by the Government of India. In formal education, to train the teachers several training colleges and DIETS have been established in each state. As a first step, these institutions must incorporate the mental retardation concepts in their training curriculum. At this stage, it is obligatory to invite and involve health and social service personnel in the development of training curricula and in the process of training the teachers. It is essential because these teachers are supposed to work in the communities apart from schools. The modern schools are not in isolation but an integral part of the community. If it is so, it is the duty of the teacher to take care of the community needs into account by formulating any curricular and co-curricular activities for children. Here is an opportunity for the teacher to generate awareness, development of positive attitudes and healthy practices in the people through Teacher-Parent Associations.

A variety of non-formal education programmes like adult education, women's education, workers education, non-formal education for girls 9-14 age group and non-formal education for 6-9 age group have been in operation in several districts of each state. Already there is a formal structure available to implement these programmes in every district. Once again there is a need to incorporate the concept of mental retardation in the training curricula of non-formal educators. While developing literate and neo-literate materials, care should be taken to incorporate mental retardation concepts in simple, practicable and understandable manner to the common public.

In urban as well as rural areas of any community, one can find Community Radio Listening Centres and Community T.V. Viewing Centres. These centres are the potential sources of dissemination of information on various aspects of mental retardation. For this purpose the All India Radio and the Doordarshan Kendras can develop Radio and TV Programmes on various aspects of mental retardation and the same can be broadcasted. If the non-formal educator working in the community is innovative in his/her approach, he or she can inform the timing and content of the programme to the general public. The public can hear and watch the programme and after the programme the non-formal educator can initiate discussion on it. Wherever there are misunderstandings about the concept, he or she can clarify the things for better sensitisation, development of proper attitudes and values, which pave way for better practices to prevent mental retardation. In this way Radio Listening Centres and TV Viewing Centres are one of the potential ways and means to overcome the problems of mental retardation. Likewise, the workers education programmes, women education programmes, women and child welfare schemes (Anganwadis) can be exploited. Better parental practices are one of the pre requisite for avoidance of mental retardation in children.

The Department of Child Development/Human Development, Social Work, Education and Health personnel must interact with the community frequently on child bearing and rearing practices, timely vaccination, the need for adequate nutritious diet for the mother and the child, toxication effects on the mother and the child, need for facilitative environment for proper mental as well as physical growth. The information on the concept, causes, characteristics, prevention and care on, mental retardation should be presented through traditional media and modern media. Banners, posters, wall newspapers, pamphlets, leaflets, harikatha, burrakatha, puppet shows, street plays etc, can be exploited in all potential ways particularly in rural areas. Audio and video cassettes can be prepared on these concepts and widely be distributed to the adult education centres and school libraries.

Every Primary Health Centre should have a guidance and counselling wing to provide guidance and counselling on genetic abnormalities. These centres are the gateways of information on mental retardation. Dietary counselling should be an integral part of the guidance and counselling programme. These centres can provide guidance on genetic disorders, consanguious marriages, teenage marriages, old age child bearing and rearing, etc. Village health inspectors and nurses should also be sensitised in this direction.

As India is having well established family planning programmes, these programmes must incorporate the mental retardation concepts and the preventive ways and means of mental retardation. Awareness should be generated on need for small family norm, timely immunization during pregnancy, vaccination for the infants, importance of breast feeding, dietary requirements during pregnancy, childbirth and motherhood.

To sum up, effective mixing and utilisation of men and materials available in different programmes and channels of disseminating information in combination of different strategies definitely facilitate to overcome the problem of mental retardation in any developed and developing countries.

Associated Problems in Mental Retardation

In addition to the deficits in intelligence and adaptive behaviour, some mentally retarded persons have medical problems or associated handicaps. Some of the common medical problems are epilepsy, hyperkinesis, physical handicaps, nutritional disorders and psychiatric problems such as autism psychosis, and neurotic disturbances.

Epilepsy

About 40 per cent of mentally retarded persons, have convulsions of one type or other. Convulsions vary in their frequency, duration and type depending upon the nature of brain damage. Fits are more common in persons with severe and profound mental retardation than those with mild or moderate mental retardation.

If a mentally retarded child is found to be having fits the following tips must be taken care.

(a) A detailed history about the fits, it's nature, duration, frequency, type, time of onset, premonitory symptoms and symptoms after fits stop, must be noticed.

(b) With all the above details the person should be referred to a doctor immediately and anti consultant medication advised by the doctor should be strictly followed.

(c) Guidance should be given to the parents regarding the person's condition, the importance of regular medication and periodical medical check-up.

(d) While training a mentally retarded person in various activities or skills, care should be taken about the occurrence of fits and the remedial measures for it.

(e) While placing the mentally retarded person proper care must be given about the nature of the job to be placed. Work places such as machinery, cutting tools, work in high buildings and near water should be avoided.

Hyperkinesis

Some of the mentally retarded children exhibit hyper kinetic behaviour. This problem occurs in child with brain damage.

The child with hyperkinesis may exhibit features such as excessively active distractible, have poor attention span, restlessness, lack of inhibition and poorly organised and poorly co-ordinated activity. They are impulsive and show fluctuations in the mood. Hyperkinetic behaviour impairs the learning process seriously. Medication is used to reduce the intensity of hyper kinetic behaviour.

Careful assessment is needed in the case of hyperkinesis because behaviour disturbances due to provoking factors in the environment. Poor parental control or lack of stimulating environment can be confused with hyperkinesis.

Psychiatric Disturbances

Some of the psychiatric disturbances in mentally retarded are autistic behaviour, psychotic states such as schizophrenia, mania and depression and neurotic states such as anxiety neurosis and hysterical neurosis. Features of autism are present in children with mental retardation whereas the psychotic and neurotic states are more common with adult mentally retarded persons.

A person with mental retardation exhibits the following symptoms.

— Remaining aloof for long periods of time

— Muttering to self and food refusal

— Unprovoked aggressive behaviour

— States of extreme elation or depression of mood

— Lack of sleep or disturbed sleep rhythm and

— Sudden change in behaviour

Multiple Handicap

An individual with more than one of the four handicaps viz. physical, hearing, vision and mental is classified under multiple handicap. Multiple handicap children grow, learn and develop more slowly than any other single handicap children. Intensive training is required even to perform the most basic skills.

Cerebral palsy with mental retardation is one of the most common form of multiple handicap. Cerebral palsy is characterized predominantly by motor disturbances and in coordination of movements of various degrees of severity. This is a non-progression condition and occurs due to damage to certain areas in the brain.

It is very difficult to identify the intensity of each of the handicaps in the multiple handicapped person. Accurate assessment of various handicaps is important in such children for developing management plan for a child.

Characteristics of Children with Mental Retardation

The characteristics of the mentally retarded persons vary depending upon the level of retardation. The terms currently used to describe the various degrees of mental retardation are mild, moderate, severe and profound. Table–2.2 describes the characteristics of persons with various degrees of mental retardation.

Table—2.2 Characteristics of Persons with Various Degrees of Mental Retardation

Descriptions	*Severity Level*			
	Mild	*Moderate*	*Severe*	*Profound*
Preschool-0-5 years	Can develop social and communication skills, minimal retardation in sensorimotor areas, often not distinguished from normal until late age.	Can talk or learn to communicate; poor social awareness; fair motor development, profits from training in self help; can be managed with moderate supervision.	Poor motor development, speech minimal; generally unable to profit from training in self-help; little or no communication skills.	Gross retardation; minimal capacity for functioning in sensori motor areas; needs nursing care.
School age—6-20 years training and education	Can learn academic skills upto approximately 6th grade level by the teens, can be guided toward social conformity.	Can profit from training in social and occupational skills; unlikely to progress beyond 2nd grade level in academic subjects; may learn to travel alone in familiar places.	Can talk or learn to communicate; can be trained in elemental health habits; profits from systematic habit training.	Some motor development present; may respond to minimal or limited training in self help.
Adult 21 and Over: Social and vocational adequacy	Can usually achieve social and vocational skills adequate to minimum self support but may need guidance and assistance when under unusual social or economic stress.	May achieve self-maintenance in unskilled or semiskilled work under sheltered conditions; needs supervision and guidance when under mild social or economic stress.	May contribute partially to self-maintenance under complete supervision; can develop self-protection skills to a minimal useful level in controlled environment.	Some motor and speech development; may achieve very limited self-care; needs nursing care.

Adapted from mental retardation activities of the US Department of Health, Education and Welfare, P. 2 United States Government Printing Office, Washington D.C., 1963. Printed in Modern Synopsis of Comprehensive text Book of Psychiatry/III Third Edition—Eds—Herold. I. Kaplan and Benjamin, J.Sadock Williams and Willikins Company—Baltimore—1981.

Every mentally retarded person may not exactly fit in the above description. There may be specific strengths and weaknesses in each person. The description of the various groups of mentally retarded persons as given in the table may sometimes overlap in a given case.

We cannot stress too strongly that individual mentally retarded children may not display all the characteristic mentioned here. There is a great deal of variability in the behaviour of retarded students, and we must consider each retarded person as a unique and separate individual. There are certain cognitive and personality characteristics of retarded individuals.

I. Cognitive Characteristics

The most obvious characteristic of retardation is a reduced ability to learn. There are a number of ways in which persons who are retarded may exhibit cognitive problems. Research has documented that retarded students are likely to have difficulties in atleast four areas related to cognition—attention, memory, language and academics.

(a) Attentional Deficits

The importance of attention for learning is critical. A child must be able to attend to the task at hand before he or she can learn it. For years researchers have posited that we can attribute many of the cognitive problems of retarded individuals to attentional problems (e.g., Brooks and McCauley, 1984; Zeamon and House, 1963). Often attending to the wrong things, many retarded people have difficulty in allocating their attention properly.

(b) Poor Memory

One of the most consistent findings in comparisons of the learning abilities of non disabled and retarded individuals is that when the latter are asked to remember a list of words or sounds or a group of pictures presented a few seconds previously, they do more poorly than the non-disabled (Borkowski, Peck, Damberg, 1983; Brown, 1974; Estes 1970).

Many authorities have conceptualised these memory problems within a theoretical framework that stresses the depth of processing that an individual must perform to remember certain material (Craik and Lockhart, 1972; Craik and Tulving, 1975). They maintain that we process incoming stimuli at various levels of analysis. At shallow levels we process only perceptual features, whereas at deeper levels we process semantic features of the incoming stimuli.

Research has demonstrated that the deeper the level of processing required, the larger the likelihood that mentally retarded individuals will have greater memory problems than their non-retarded peers (Schultz, 1983). In other words, the more complicated the memory task, the more likely it is that a retarded individual will have difficulties with it.

One of the primary reasons for the problems of the retarded individuals regarding, complicated memory tasks is that they have difficulty in using efficient learning strategies such as mediation and organization (Borkowski and Wanschura, 1974; Bray, 1979; Brown, 1974). An example of a mediation strategy is rehearsal. When given a list of words to remember, most individuals will rehearse the list aloud or to themselves in an attempt to "keep" the words in memory. Retarded students generally do not use rehearsal spontaneously (Borkowski and Cavanaugh, 1979).

Many authorities have attributed retarded students efficient use of learning strategies such as rehearsal and clustering to the fact that their executive control processes are less well developed (Brown, 1974; Justice, 1985; Sternberg and Spear, 1985). Executive control processes, also called metacognitive processes, "are used to plan how to solve a problem, to monitor one's solution strategy as it is being executed, and to evaluate the results of this strategy once it has been implemented". (Sternberg and Spear 1985, p.303). Research has demonstrated that when confronted with learning problems, retarded individuals frequently have trouble in picking the best strategies to use, monitoring the use of the strategies (keeping track of their own performance) and evaluating the use of strategies (knowing whether the strategies are working). Research has shown that they can be taught to use spontaneous use of learning strategies and executive control processes successfully (Glidden, 1985).

(c) Language Developmental Delay

Many mentally retarded individuals have language and speech problems. Such as articulation errors. Mildly retarded individuals follow the same developmental course in language development but their language development progresses at slower rate. Severely retarded children exhibit inadequate language development.

(d) Poor Academic Achievement

There is a lag behind their non-retarded peer in all the areas of achievement because there is strong relationship between intelligence and achievement. They also tend to be underachievers in relation to expectations based on their intellectual level (Mac Millan, 1982).

Their learning depends more on rote memory than on understanding. They repeat the errors again and again because of rote memory. They find difficulty in abstract and critical thinking, employing critical judgement, avoiding errors, and in exercising foresight. All these factors contribute to their poor academic performance.

Personality Characteristics

(a) Social and Emotional Inadequacy

Mentally retarded individuals are candidates for a variety of social and emotional problems. In particular, they often have problems in making friends (Luftig, 1988; Zetlin and Murtaugh, 1988) and have poor self-concepts (Leahy, Balla, and Zigler, 1982). There are at least two reasons why this may be so. First, some of their behaviour may "turn off" their peers. For ex; they engage in higher rates of inattention and disruptive behaviour than their non- retarded classmates. Second, their non-retarded peers may shun them simply because they do not want to associate with people who are disabled. In either case, they end up having problems in social interactions with others.

(b) Lack of Motivation

In addition to social-emotional problems, and perhaps to some degree because of these difficulties many persons who are retarded have motivational problems (Balla and Zigler, 1979;

Zigler and Balla, 1982). They tend to lack confidence in their own abilities. Believing that they have little control over what happens to them and that they are primarily controlled by other people or events, they have a tendency to give up early when faced with challenging tasks.

(c) Limited Individual Differences

No two individuals in this world have similar personality. But in the code of mentally retarded children there appear to be less prominent individual differences. As non-retarded children the retarded children do not exhibit such masked individual differences. It is rare to find individuals who may be described as dynamic, charming, forceful, vicious, obnoxious or outstanding. Many mentally retarded children are colourless and tractable.

(d) Organism Inferiority

Mentally retarded children suffer from general structural and functional inferiority of the entire organism. These children learn to talk and wait at a much later stage. Defective speech and shuffling gait are two very prominent characteristics of these children. Sensory discrimination is less acute for the retarded children when compared with non-retarded children. The retardates are relatively insensitive to pain and their auditory and visual defects are common.

(e) Adjustment Problem

Mentally retarded children experience mild depression, feelings of worthless and helplessness. Retarded children feel angry and rebellious because of frustration of psychological, and social needs. Over protection by the parents do not encourage learning self-help skills. This type of behaviour fosters a dependent style of interaction in the retardation. This over protection and denial of the parents results in adjustment difficulties of such type of children.

Summary

To sum up, this chapter dealt with the factors such as— biological factors, psycho-social factors, organic risk factors, polygenic inheritance and psycho-social/cultural influences. Genetic abnormalities like Down Syndrome, Fragile × Syndrome and Williams Syndrome exhibit clinical features resulting in mental retardation. Prenatal and birth complications or perinatal factors also contribute for mental retardation. Malnutrition of mother, exposure to disease, chemicals, drugs and x-rays, low birth weight and pre-maturity are also associated with neurological and intellectual deficits. Forceps delivery, head injury and anoxia also take a toll. Various postnatal factors may also result in mental retardation. Seizures, brain tumors, infections, encephalitis, and meningitis are also some of the factors that cause mental retardation.

Polygenic inheritance also influences intelligence in normal populations. Psycho-social factors such as malnutrition, inadequate, medical and prenatal care, disease proned conditions, child rearing practices, home environment, family structures influence intelligence level may result in mental retardation. Mild mental retardation caused by psycho-social factors is almost always difficult to identify in young children. Stimulating environment has positive influence in the development of intelligence level.

Causative factors for mental retardation can be categorised into prenatal, perinatal and postnatal causes. Preventive measures like genetic counselling, chronic villus sampling, amniocentesis, sonography immunization for pregnant women and for the infant, periodic medical check up etc, were explained. Precautions to be taken if mentally retarded children have fits are also discussed. Hyperkinesis behaviours such as excessive active, distractible, poor attention, impulsiveness impairs learning process. Psychiatric disturbances and multiple handicaps are also present in mentally retarded children.

Mentally retarded children exhibit cognitive deficits, attentional deficits, poor memory, language development delay, poor academic achievement, lack of motivation, limited individual differences, organism inferiority, and adjustment problems. These are some of the characteristics exhibited by the mentally retarded individual.

3

Early Identification and Intervention

OBJECTIVES

This chapter aims to present various modes of identification and intervention programmes for mentally retarded children. After reading this chapter you should be able to:

1. List out the various tests used for identification of mentally retarded children;
2. Know different aspects to be kept in mind in assessment and intervention;
3. Skill in developing intervention programmes and ways to train mentally retarded children.

Introduction

For educational intervention programmes, early identification and assessment form a foundation. Identification is the process of establishing an awareness that a problem exists (Hayden and Edgar, 1977). Certain kinds of problems or potential problems can be identified very early. For e.g., conditions such as Tay Sachs disease and Down's syndrome may be detected during pregnancy by amniocentesis. This procedure involves testing the amniotic fluid surrounding the foetus to determine whether a problem exists. Beck (1977) stated that 6.8 per cent of all handicapped children could and should be identified at birth or shortly after birth. Conditions identifiable at birth by urine tests are genetic disorders such as galactosemia and phenylketonuria (PKU). Early intervention for such conditions is possible by intake of special diets for the infants. In the period between birth and school age, there are procedures to identify children who need special services, but they are not universally applied (Kakalik, Brewer, Dougherty, Fleischauer and Genensky, 1973). Early identification helps a teacher to identify the abilities and disabilities severity and to plan early intervention programme based on the current performance and ability of a child. For identifying children with mental retardation, one has to screen and assess the intelligence level (IQ) and the adaptive behaviour. These two factors should be assessed with the help of various standardized tests. Based on the IQ level and adaptive behaviour score, the intervention programme and placement can be arrived at. To be classified as mentally retarded, a child must be unable to demonstrate behaviour based on intellectual functioning that is appropriate for that person's age or social situation (Salvia, 1978). For the special education teacher it seems appropriate to define intelligence in terms of children's interactions with their environment: how well they meet the demands made on them by their school, family, community and other social institutions.

To identify mental retardation assessment of intelligence, adaptive behaviour and academic achievement along with a developmental history may be more than sufficient for diagnosis. Assessment of intelligence, adaptive behaviour, behaviour adjustment and problems, academic progress, family functioning and medical concerns are all appropriate depending upon the case.

In identification and assessment, the two main criteria given by the American Association of Mental Retardation (AMMR) to define and diagnose mental retardation are sub-average intellectual functioning and problems of social adaptive behaviour. Using a single test or scale cannot assess the intellectual functioning and adaptive behaviour of mentally retarded. More than one test is needed for providing a reliable and fair evaluation of the mentally retarded person. There are three important areas of assessment in mentally retarded. They are:

1. Measurement of the overall level of 'General Intellectual Functioning'.

2. Assessment of 'Adaptive Behaviour'.
3. Detailed Analysis of Individual abilities and deficits.

Assessment based on Developmental Milestones of the Child

In the early year's, identification of milestones of the child will also form the part and parcel of screening and assessment. A normal developmental milestone is an aid for identifying delayed development. Normal developmental milestones and the appropriate age of their attainment relevant to Indian situations are given below. Some children may skip few of the stages.

S. No.	*Milestones*	*Age*
1.	Smiles at others	4 months
2.	Holds head erect	4 months
3.	Puts objects into mouth	4 months
4.	Rolls from back on to stomach	6 months
5.	Uses whole palm to grasp	7 months
6.	Makes sounds anna and dadda	7 months
7.	Sits without support	8 months
8.	Responds to name	10 months
9.	Crawls	10 months
10.	Stands by holding on to an object	10 months
11.	Holds object with thumb and index finger	10 months
12.	Stands without support	10 months
13.	Says "amma", "akka", "atta" meaningfully	15 months
14.	Walks without support	15 months
15.	Tells own name	18 months
16.	Drinks by self with a glass	21 months
17.	Shows body parts when named	24 months
18.	Indicates toilet needs	24 months
19.	Speaks in small sentences	30 months
20.	Unbuttons clothes	36 months
21.	Gives meaningful verbal answers to simple questions	36 months
22.	Differentiates big and small	36 months
23.	Identifies boy or girl	36 months
24.	Can button clothes	40 months
25.	Combs hair	48 months

* (Based on the survey carried out by NIMH team, Mental Retardation-Manual for Psychologists, 1989).

PICTORIAL REPRESENTATION OF NORMAL DEVELOPMENTAL MILESTONES IN CHILDREN

1. Smiles at others
4 months

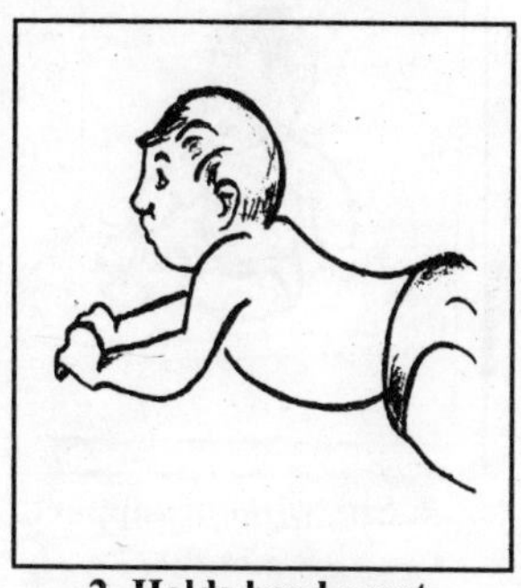

2. Holds head erect
4 months

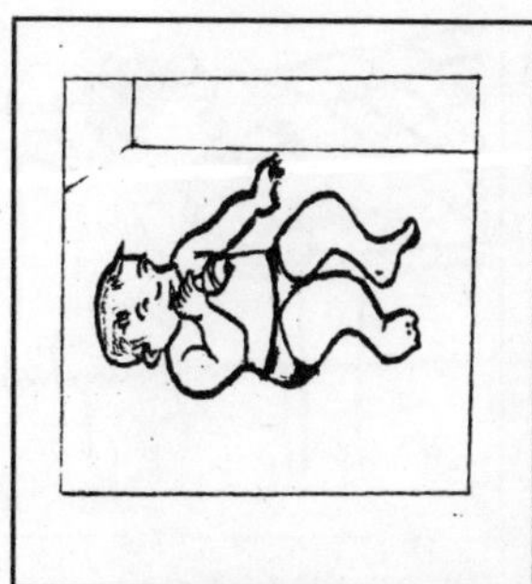

3. Put objects into mouth
4 months

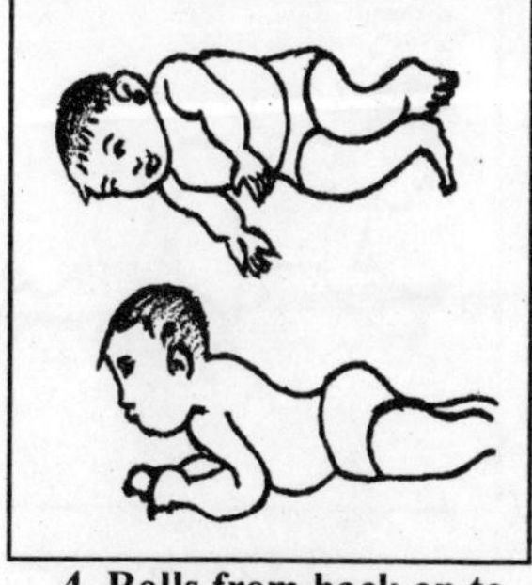

4. Rolls from back on to stomach
6 months

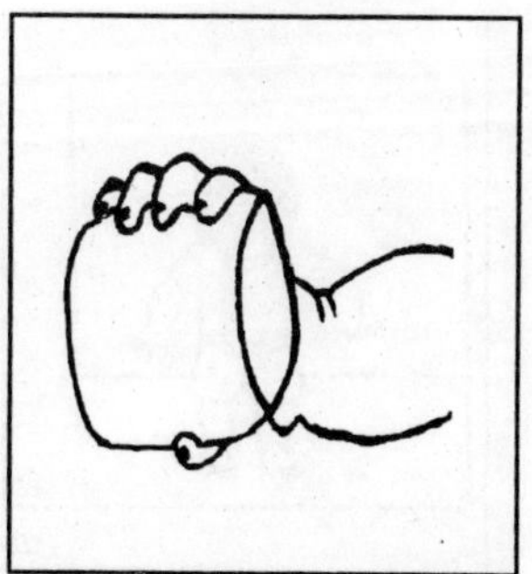

5. Uses whole palm to grasp
7 months

6. Makes sounds 'amma' 'da...da'
7 months

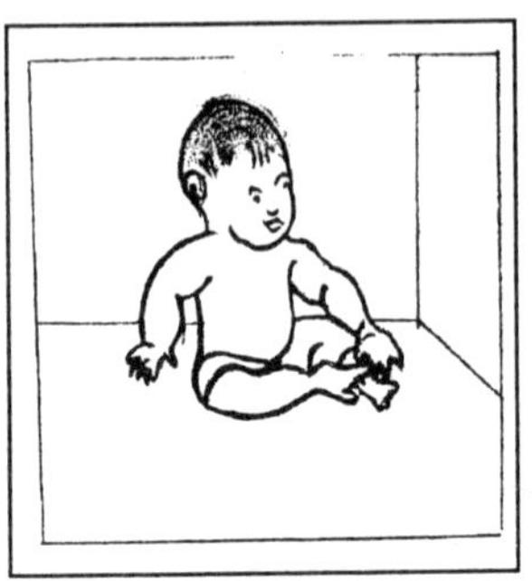

7. Sits without support
8 months

8. Response to name
10 months

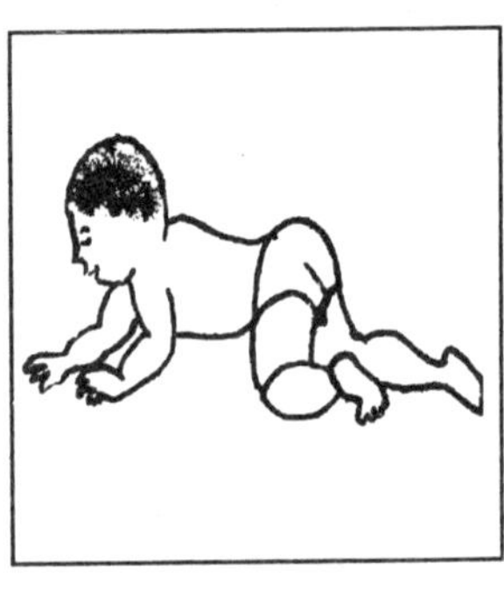

9. Crawls
10 months

10. Stands by holding onto
an object
10 months

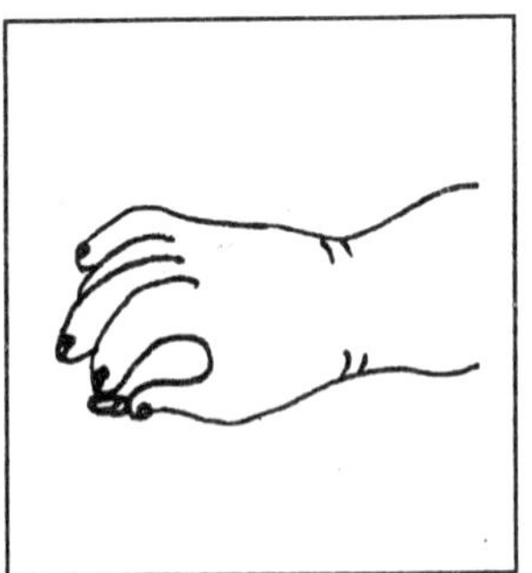

11. Holds an object with
thumb and index finger
10 months

12. Stands without support
10 months

13. Says 'amma', 'akka' meaningfully
15 months

14. Walks without support
15 months

15. Tells own name
18 months

16. Drinks by self with a glass
21 months

17. Shows body parts when named.
24 months

18. Indicate toilet needs
24 months

19. Speaks in small sentences
30 months

20. Unbuttons clothes
36 months

21. Gives meaningful verbal answers to simple questions
36 months

22. Differentiates big and small
36 months

23. Identifies boy or girl
36 months

24. Can button clothes
40 months

25. Combs hair
48 months

Early identification of mental retardation is made by seeing how much a child is delayed on the milestones of development. Identification of mental retardation is done by using certain questionnaire or checklists called screening schedules. There are three screening schedules given below. The first is for the children below 3 years of age. The second for those between 3-6 years of age. The third is for those aged 7 years and above. Age range has to be taken into consideration while screening for developmental delays. Age range is given in the screening schedule.

Screening Schedule No. I (Below 3 Years)

S. No.	*Item*	*Normal age Range*	*Milestone delay if not achieved*
1.	Responds to name/voice	1-3 months	4th months
2.	Smiles at others	1-4 months	6th months
3.	Holds head steady	2-6 months	6th months
4.	Sits without support	5-10 months	12th months
5.	Stands without support	9-14 months	18th months
6.	Walks well	10-20 months	20th months
7.	Talks in 2-3 word sentences	16-30 months	3rd years
8.	Eats/drinks by self	2-3 years	4th years
9.	Tells his name	2-3 years	4th years
10.	Has toilet control	3-4 years	4th years
11.	Avoids simple hazards	3-4 years	4th years
12.	Has fits	Yes	No
13.	Has physical disabilities	Yes	No

If the child is found to be delayed in any one of the items given from S.No. 1-11 and with fits or physical disability, then the child is suspected for mental retardation.

Screening Schedule No. II (3 to 6 years)

Observe the following:

1. Compared with other children, did the child have any serious delay in sitting, standing or walking? Yes/No
2. Does the child appear to have difficulty in hearing. Yes/No
3. Does the child have difficulty in seeing. Yes/No
4. When you tell, the child to do something, does he seem to have problems in understanding what you are saying. Yes/No
5. Does the child have weakness and/or stiffness in the limbs and/or difficulty in walking or moving his arms? Yes/No
6. Does the child sometimes have fits, become rigid, or lose consciousness? Yes/No
7. Dose the child have difficulty in learning to do things like other children of his age? Yes/No
8. Is the child not able to speak at all? (Cannot make himself understood in words/say any recognisable words). Yes/No
9. Is the child's speech in any way different from normal (not clear enough to be understood by people other than his immediate family?) Yes/No
10. Compared to other children of his age, does the child appear in any way backward, dull or slow? Yes/No

---

* If any of the above items is answered 'Yes', suspect mental retardation.

* Adapted from the International Pilot study of Severe Childhood Disability-Final Report—Screening for Severe Mental Retardation in developing countries.

Screening Schedule No. III (7 years and above)

1. When compared with other children, did the child have any serious delay in sitting, standing or walking? Yes/No
2. When the child not does things for himself like eating, dressing and grooming? Yes/No
3. Whether the child have difficulty in understanding when you say do this or that. Yes/No
4. Whether the child's speech not unclear? Yes/No
5. Whether the child have difficulty in expressing without being asked the child has seen/heard? Yes/No

6. If the child have fits, become rigid or loss consciousness. Yes/No
7. Compared to other children of his age, does the child appear in the way backward, dull or slow? Yes/No

If any one of the above items is answered 'Yes' suspect mental retardation.

Some questions in Screening Schedules II and III are over inclusive. Those with physical handicap or epilepsy alone without mental retardation can be spotted. These two screening schedules are prompt identification of every single mentally retarded child.

Psychological testing is also very important in addition to the diagnostic function based on developmental milestones, because:

1. It provides a profile of abilities and disabilities of the mentally retarded, which helps in training;
2. Helps to evaluate the effects of therapeutic intervention by measuring change overtime;
3. Prognostic information about the potentialities of the mentally retarded can be identified by psychological assessment;
4. Aptitude tests and interest inventories combined with intelligence tests will be useful while planning vocational training for mentally retarded.

I. Tests for Assessing General Intelligence in Mental Retardation

The most commonly used tests may be classified into three types:

1. Developmental schedules for infants and pre-school children;
2. Verbal tests;
3. Non-verbal and performance tests.

1. Developmental Schedules

These are based on observation of the development of sensory-motor activity in infants and pre-school children. The obtained developmental quotients (DQ) are known to correlate poorly with IQs measured later in life. In assessing the developmental level of children upto five years of age, developmental schedules are very useful as screening instruments.

Gesell's Developmental Schedule (GDS, 1941) is the most commonly used developmental schedules. This schedule yields scores on four areas of development.

1. Motor behaviour
2. Adaptive behaviour
3. Language and
4. Personal and social behaviour.

Gesell's developmental schedule is given in Appendix—1.

2. Verbal Tests

These tests involve the predominant use of language and oral items. The measures for verbal test are calculated in terms of IQ whereas on performance tests are given as performance quotients (PQ).

The Stanford-Binet Test-SBT (1905) is a commonly used verbal test. This test is revised and adapted to Indian conditions and is available as Binet-Kamat test. This test is extensively used verbal test for mentally retarded persons from 3 years to 22 years. It provides a pattern analysis for seven primary abilities namely—language, memory, conceptual thinking, reasoning, numerical reasoning, visual-motor co-ordination and social intelligence.

Verbal intelligence tests in various Indian languages (Marathi, Gujarathi, Kannada and Hindi) based on Stanford-Binet test have been found to be valid and reliable. Items in this test are either oral or simple manipulative tasks like drawing, writing and following simple instructions.

3. Non-Verbal and Performance Tests

In this test subjects express their answers in the form of drawing, gestures, activities such as arranging blocks and puzzles, matching designs and placing pictures meaningfully. Non-verbal tests are culture fair. They require minimal dependence on past experience. Mentally retarded persons with speech and hearing problems or with limited verbal abilities would be at disadvantage on verbal tests and have to be assessed on appropriate performance or non-verbal tests.

The Seguin Form Board Test (SFB) and Gesell's Drawing Test are some of the performance tests. This tests serves as a quick measures of general intelligence. Alexander's Pass Along Test and Koh's Block Design Test are performance tests, which can be administered on persons with mild mental retardation. Performance test measures only certain aspects of intelligence such as motor activity, visual motor perception or spatial abilities. Therefore for assessment of general intelligence, performance test should be used with non-verbal tests such as Raven's Progressive Matrices.

(a) Seguin Form Board Test (1876)

This test is commonly used performance test for measuring psychomotor and visuo-perceptual abilities of children between four to twenty years. The instruction for administration and norms for SFB are given in the Appendix—II.

(b) Developmental Screening Test (DST-Bharatraj)

This is a non-verbal test designed to measure the mental development of children from birth to 15 years. The information is obtained by the use of a semi-structured interview with the parents/care takers without requiring the use of performance on any of the tasks. This screening test is carried out for assessing children who are non-co-operative, those with multiple impairments or those with severe behaviour problems making the test batteries unsuitable. Developmental Screening Test details are given in Appendix—III.

(c) Malin's Intelligence Scale for Indian Children (MISIC)

This test is an adaptation of Weschler's Intelligence Scale for children. The sub tests of MISIC provide overall (Intelligence Quotient) and PQ (Performance Quotient) and profiles of different abilities in the person.

II. Assessment of Adaptive Behaviour

Adaptive behaviour is the functional ability of the individual to acquire personal independence and social responsibility. Effective coping with the natural and social demands of the environment by an individual is the social adaptability. In 1935, Doll introduced the concept of assessing adaptive behaviour with the Genetic Scale of Social Maturity, which Doll originally developed to assess children and adults with mental retardation. Sparrow, Balla and Cicchetti published the current revision of the instrument, the Vineland Social Maturity Scale (VSMS) in 1984. American Association on Mental Retardation Adaptive Behaviour Scale (1975) is also one of the most commonly used scales for assessing adaptive behaviour of the mentally retarded persons.

(a) Vineland Social Maturity Scale-VSMS (1984)

Vineland Social Maturity Scale (VSMS-Sparrow et al. 1984) has been adapted for Indian population. This scale is useful in assessing severely mentally retarded individuals who cannot cope with formal testing procedures. Semi-structured interviews with the child or guardian/caretakers are conducted to collect data. VSMS gives a profile on development in eight areas viz, self help general, self help eating, self help dressing, self direction, socialisation, occupation, communication and locomotion. With the help of VSMS, social age and social quotients (SQ) can be computed from the individuals scores. The VSMS is given in Appendix-IV.

(b) American Association on Mental Deficiency Adaptive Behaviour Scale

The AMMD Adaptive Behaviour Scale (AAMD-ABS-Nihira, Foster, Shellhass and Leland, 1975) measures the personal and social performance of individuals with mental retardation who live in institutional settings. The American Association on Mental Deficiency Adaptive Behaviour Scale-School Edition (ABS-SE) measures the personal independence, personality and behaviour disorders of students from age 3 to 16 years. Special educators use the ABS-SE to help in diagnosing and classifying children with disabilities, especially mental retardation. This scale gives a quantitative description of the coping behaviour of the mentally retarded individuals. The ABS-SE is arranged in 2 domains and is further divided into the 21 sub-domains. The first domain covers the levels of development in ten areas of functioning such as:

1. Personal dependence in daily living
2. Independent functioning
3. Physical development
4. Economic activity
5. Language development
6. Numbers and time
7. Pre vocational activity
8. Self direction
9. Responsibility and
10. Socialisation

Second domain is concerned with maladaptive behaviour under 14 different categories.

1. Personality and behaviour disorders
2. Aggressiveness
3. Anti-social Vs Social Behaviour
4. Rebelliousness
5. Trust worthiness
6. Withdrawal Vs Involvement
7. Mannerisms
8. Interpersonal manners
9. Acceptability of vocal habits
10. Acceptability of habits
11. Activity level
12. Symptomatic behaviour and
13. Use of medications

The scale allows a profile of skills and behaviour problems to be concentrate for each individual. Details of VSMS and some of the items of AAMR adaptive behaviour scale are given in Appendix—VI.

III. Assessment of Specific Abilities and Deficits

This assessment of specific abilities helps in the planning of the training programmes. Assessment should be done on gross and fine motor skills, visuo-spatial abilities, language abilities, verbal and non-verbal communication and attention span. Knox cube Imitation test and digit Span and cancellation tests are used to assess attention span.

Child with brain damage has deficits in visuo-perceptual, spatial and visuo-motor abilities. Some of the tests used to assess such child are:

I. Bender Gestalt test

II. Benton Visual Retention test

III. Draw-a-man test.

Subtests of Stanford-Binet test, Malin's Intelligence Scale for Indian children and Gesell's Developmental Schedules are able to assess cognitive abilities whereas, the VSMS and AAMR adaptive behaviour scale assess adaptive behaviour. The results from these tests also give the pattern of specific abilities and deficits in a child.

Some Tests Used for Mentally Retarded Persons

1. Developmental Schedules

Bayley Infant Scales (Bayley, 1969)

Gessell's Developmental Schedules (Gessell, 1941)

NIMH Developmental Assessment Schedule (1989)

2. Verbal Tests

1. Binet-Kamat Test (Kannada, Marathi)
2. Binet-Kulshresta Test (Hindi)
3. Binet-Shukla Test (Gujarati)

4. Malin's Intelligence Scale for Indian Children-verbal Scale.

3. Non-Verbal Test

5. Developmental Screening tests
6. Raven's Progressive matrices-Coloured (Raven, Court and Raven, 1985)

4. Performance Test

7. Seguin Form Board Test (1876)
8. Gessell's Drawing Test
9. Draw-a-men Test
10. Malin's Intelligence Scale for Indian Children-Performance Scale
11. Alexander's pass along Test
12. Koh's Block Design Test

5. Adaptive Behaviour Scales

13. Vineland Social Maturity Scale (1984)
14. American Association of Mental Retardation Adaptive Behaviour Scale (1975)

6. Tests for Specific Abilities

15. Attention-Concentration Tests (Digit Span, Cancellation, Knox-cube test)
16. Tests of perception (Bender Gestalt tests, Benton Visual retention tests).

There are so many problems specific to the assessment of mentally retarded. They are:

1. The mental retarded children may have multisensory and impairments like loss of vision, hearing and deficits in gross and fine motor skills. This can substantially affect test performance and the resultant IQ scores.
2. The mental retarded children may have severe delay in language development affecting their expressive

and receptive speech as well as all forms of communication—verbal and non-verbal. Their comprehension of test instructions may be limited.

3. Hyperactivity, aggressiveness, social withdrawal etc. may make the child difficult to assess according to standard testing procedures.

4. Some of the mentally retarded individuals have poor attention and high distractibility and hence testing will be difficult.

5. Peer motivation and co-operation also affect test performance.

As there is no single test applicable to all mentally retarded with or without the associated problems, the choice of the right tests becomes very important.

Different Aspects to be Kept in Mind in Assessment and Intervention

To delineate a management programme or to develop early intervention programme for a child it is essential that his/her strengths and weaknesses are found out. This is done by assessing his present level of functioning. Assessment means finding the capability of a mentally retarded child at any time to identify his/her placement/position/level in various skills. For example, one should first know whether a mentally retarded child could hold a pencil before teaching him how to write. Assessment of the ability to grasp the pencil is necessary. The level of performance of the mentally retarded child must be assessed in the following developmental areas.

1. Vision and hearing (sensory ability)
2. Gross and fine motor ability
3. Self care ability
4. Language ability
5. Cognitive ability
6. Social and emotional ability

Assessment should be carried out in a systematic way and in the same order as the development of the child. Assessment should be based on definite and exact fact either observed or supplied by the informers. The assessment should not be based on guess or probabilities. While assessing the child in all areas, the child should be compared with an average normal child of the same age. This comparison helps us to know how far mentally retarded child lags behind.

Early Intervention

One of the most dramatic studies of the long-range effectiveness of early intervention was designed by Skeels and Dye (1939) and followed up by Skeels (1966). The plan for the study came from an accidental discovery of IQ gains in two young "hopeless" children institutionalised with older retarded women who cared for them and played with them. The study was severely criticised, but it is recognised today as one of the earliest empirical studies of the effectiveness of early intervention.

Early identification helps us to develop early intervention programme or management plan for mentally retarded child.

The management plan of the mentally retarded child depends upon the current level of functioning of the child and the associated conditions such as epilepsy, hyperkinesis, behaviour problems and sensory handicaps. The early intervention varies from infant stimulation, developing daily living skills and functional academics to pre-vocational and vocational skills. Early intervention programme should also concentrate on speech, locomotion, management of problematic behaviour and managing medical problems.

Once a mentally retarded child's current level of functioning is established, a programme appropriate for him/his must be developed. In other words, Individualised Education Programme (IEP) is planned to provide appropriate education and training for the mentally retarded children. IEP plan should depend upon the needs of each mentally retarded child. Physiotherapy, speech therapy, occupational therapy and behaviour therapy with basic reading and writing skills should be the part and parcel of the individualised education programme.

Therefore, IEP is a team effort of the personnel—physiotherapist, speech pathologist, psychologist, occupational therapist and special educators.

The components of the IEP are:

(1) Current level of functioning of the child in specific skills, (2) Annual goals, (3) Short term objectives, (4) Methods of training, (5) Materials required to train, (6) Persons who would train, (7) Duration, (8) Terminal behaviour and (9) Evaluation for further programme planning.

Such an IEP is very essential in teaching the retarded children because no two retarded children can be taught the same programme. Each child differs from others with his/her needs, strengths and weaknesses. So the programme developed should be tailored to suit the needs of each child. After developing IEP divide the task/activity into small sequential steps and demonstrate and training that particular step. This is known as task analysis. Regular, systematic and repeated training with reinforcement will lead to a progress in the child. Effective intervention involves various steps, which is given in the form of flow chart.

Steps for Developing Effective Intervention Programme

1. Selecting skill for training mentally retarded children.
2. The skill should be divided into small sequential steps.
3. Repeated training in each activity is given according to his/her ability level.
4. Systematic and regular training should be given to the child to progress in its own pace.
5. Training should start with what the child already knows and then proceed to the skill that needs to be trained. This makes the child to feel his/her success and achievement.

Various Steps in Intervention Training Programme for Mentally Retarded

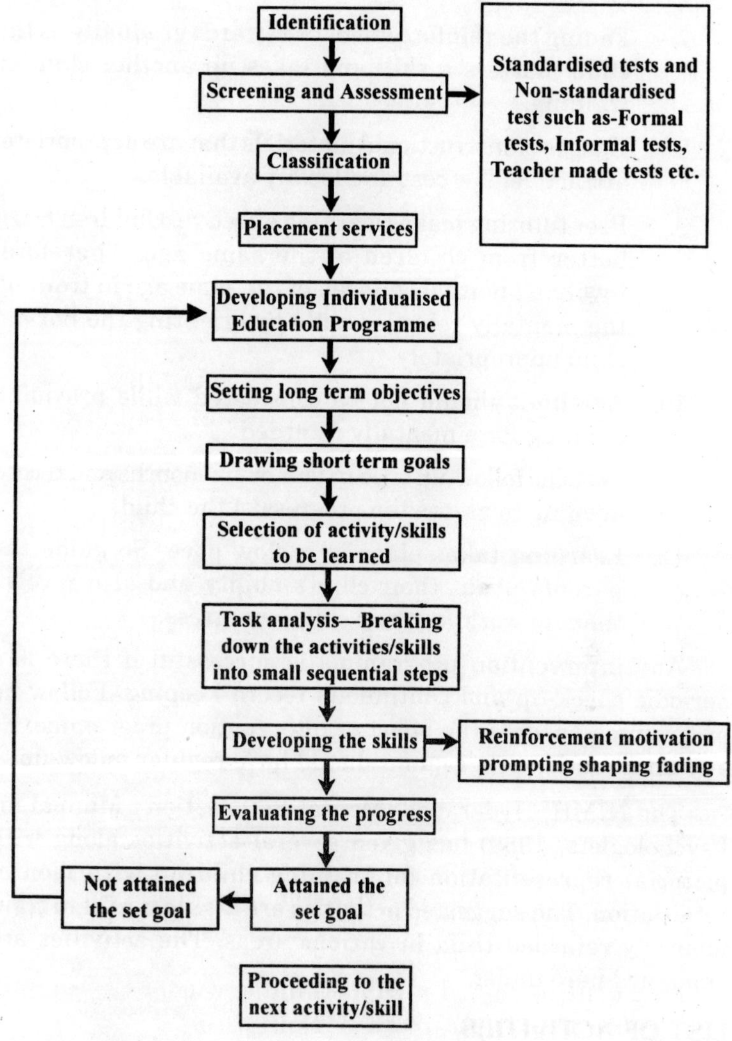

6. Reinforcement even for near success by appreciation or with some objects that he likes will increase the effort.
7. Fading the reinforcement or rewards gradually as the child masters a skill and takes up another skill for training.
8. Usages of instructional materials that are appropriate, attractive, low cost and locally available.
9. Peer tutoring makes learning effective. Children learn better from children of the same age. Therefore, involving normal children of the same age in training the mentally retarded child by orienting the normal child appropriately.
10. Age limit should not be considered while providing training for a mentally retarded.
11. Periodic follow-up once in four or six months and record keeping to assess the progress of the child.
12. Learning takes place in a slow pace. So guide the parents about their child's ability and also involve them to work for their child's progress.

Any intervention programme is successful if there is a periodic check-up and continuous record keeping. Follow-up programme ensures the effect of intervention programme. So any intervention programme should have regular follow-up.

The NIMH, Hyderabad (Mental Retardation : Manual for Psychologists, 1989) has given several activities along with pictorial representation for training children with mental retardation. The suggested activities are highly useful to train mentally retarded child in various areas. The activities are explained here under.

LIST OF ACTIVITIES

Activity—1

To make the child smile in response to facial expression of others.

1. Bend your head slightly above the child's face to catch his look, talk to him and smile.
2. Talk and smile when you are feeding him, giving bath to him, dressing him and so on.
3. Respond by smiling whenever he smiles.
4. Smile at him whenever you pick him up and play with him.

Activity—2

To make the child hold his head erect when placed on his abdomen on a flat surface.

Materials—A Rattle/Toy, Cylindrical Pillow

1. Keep a pillow under his arms and chest (as shown in picture). Hold a colourful toy in front of the child and let him look at it.
2. Place the child on his stomach without the pillow. Rest his elbows on the floor. Physically guide the child to lift his hand and look up. Gradually reduce support.

Activity—3

To make the child say: 'Ma-Ma', 'Ap Pa'-'Ya-Ya', etc.

Materials-Sugar syrup, Honey

1. Keep the child in such a position that he can look at your face. Make sounds like 'Ma-Ma', 'Ap-pa', 'Ya-Ya' and so on repeatedly. Let him try to reproduce the sounds.
2. When the child responds to your talking by vocalising, carefully apply sugar syrup/honey behind his upper teeth. The child would start licking and in the process would make sounds like 'Ma-Ma' 'Ap-Pa, and 'Ya-Ya', etc.

Activity—4

To make the child roll from his back on to the stomach.

Materials : Colourful toys, Pillows.

1. Show colourful toys to attract him on his side just above his head.
2. When the child is on his back hold his leg and hand of the same side and gently roll him over. Reduce the help gradually.
3. Make him lie sideways keep a pillow to support him at the back and gently push the pillow so that he turns and reaches for the toys.

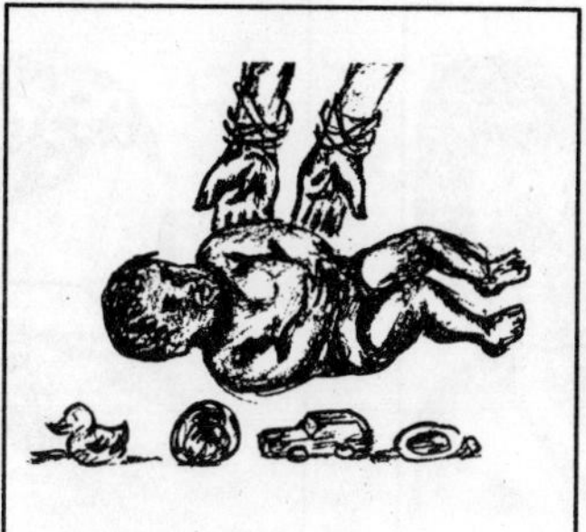

Activity—5

To make the child use his whole palm to grasp.

Materials: A toy or a biscuit to fit in child's palm (The child can be lying on his back or setting in your lap).

1. Place a toy/biscuit in the child's hand. Tell him to hold it. If the grip is not tight, hold his fist with your hand. Slowly release the pressure of your hand and finally, take away your hand.
2. Place maida paste at the lower part of the child's palm. Place a small toy in the centre of his palm and fold his fingers so that his fingers touch the paste. He can hold a toy for a few seconds because the finger gets stick to the lower part of the palm.

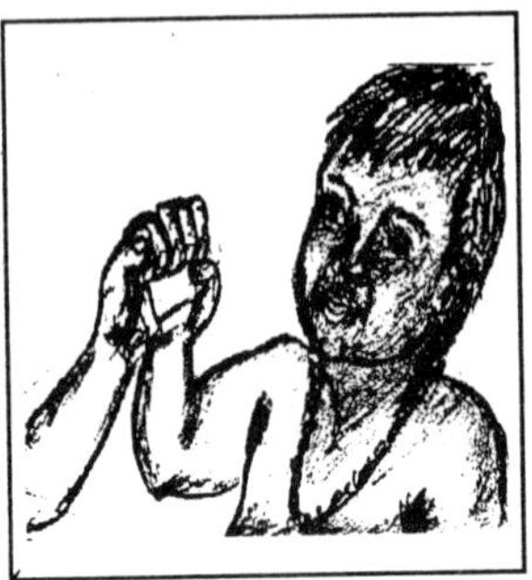

Activity—6

To make the child respond to his name.

Materials : A mirror

1. Call the child by name during various activities such as feeding him, bathing him, changing of his clothes and playing with him.
2. Show him his image in the mirror and say his name. Ask 'where is..... (name of the child).
3. Physically guide his hand to his chest and say "here is ______ (name)". While looking into the mirror.
4. Always use a single name and encourage the family members to call him by that name while talking to him.

Activity—7

To make the child sit without support

Materials-Pillow and toys, cardboard box. (Select the activity depending upon the requirement of the child).

1. Place the child on his back and hold his fingers tight and pull him upto-sitting position. See that his legs are stretched and slightly spread apart to get the balance. Support the back with your palm and slowly reduce the support. Keep toys in front of the child so that the child is busy with them.
2. Keep the pillows at the back of the child to support him in sitting position. Gradually remove pillows one by one so that the child sits without the support. Always keep some toys in front of the child and/or see that some other child plays with the child.
3. In a cardboard box make the child sit in a corner. The height of the box should reach the shoulders of the child while sitting. Gradually, reduce his height to under arms, to the waist and finally remove the box.
4. Make the child sit in the corner of a room. Keep colourful toys in front of him. Keep talking to him.

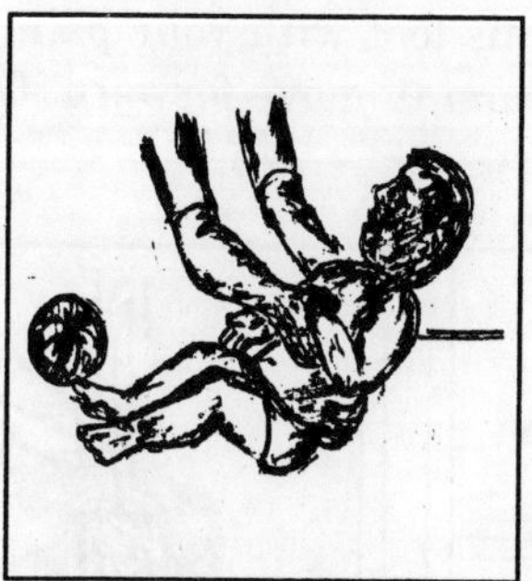

Activity—8

To make the child to crawl.

Materials: Toys, Eatables.

1. Place the child on his stomach and place some toys few inches away from his reach. Get his attention by tapping the toy on the floor and tell him to take it. Gradually increase the distance between the toy/ eatables and the child.
2. Make the child rest his palm and knees on the floor. Run a towel under the child's chest and abdomen. Lift the ends of the towel so that the child's trunk is raised. Make him crawl towards the toys in front of him.
3. Support the sole of his foot with your palm. He will push against your palm to move forward. Gradually withdraw the support.

Activity—9

To make the child stand by holding on to an object.

Materials: Toys, Table/Cot

1. Show a toy to the child and place the toy on a low table/cot while the child watches. Encourages him to hold the table top or cot, pull himself up to reach the toy. Push at the hip to make the child stand.
2. Make sure that the child is able to place both his/her feet on the ground by holding him/her under the arms and making him stand.

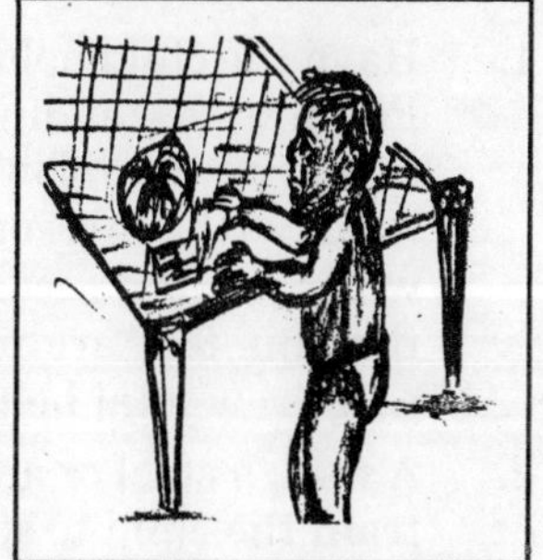

Activity—10

To make the child pick up an object with his thumb and his index finger.

Materials: Pieces of chapati, fluffed rice, gum.

1. Give small chapatti pieces to the child. Encourage him to pick them up with his thumb and his index finger and let him eat.

2. Place small bits of eatables on a plate and physically help him pick up a piece with his thumb and his index finger and eat. Gradually reduce the help.

3. Place some honey or a sticky edible on the child's thumb and his index finger. Press them a couple of times. When the gum dries the child needs to make an effort to pull the fingers apart. It becomes a play and the child keeps trying it. If needed, help him physically.

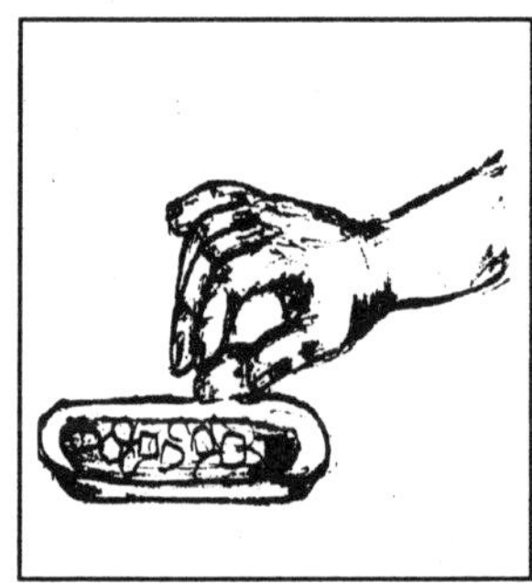

Activity—11

To make the child stand without support.

1. Have the child hold your fingers with both his hands. Pull him to standing position and keep talking to him as you do this, slowly withdraw one hand and let him hold with only one hand and stand. Gradually withdraw the second hand also. Let him stand. See that his feet are placed apart to balance when you withdraw total help.

2. A wall, a stool or any such support can also be used to train the child to stand.

Activity—12

To make the child say 'amma', 'akka' (meaningful terms, kinship terms).

Materials: Photograph of relatives

1. Point of the child's mother, brother or sister and ask- "who is this?" Give the answer and let the child imitate. Reward the child even if the child makes an attempt or approximation. In a group of persons ask the child "where is ....?" and point to that person and say "there is ....?".
2. Show a photograph of his nearest relative with whom he spends most of the time and let the child point at that person. Give the name of the person (akka/anna/amma), and let the child repeat the name.
3. Let a relative stand infront of the child. Let the child touch/point at that person and say the name of the relative.

Activity—13

To make the child walk without help.

Materials: A three wheeled cart (Walker), Toys.

1. Stand behind the child and support the child at the shoulders. Place your toes at the heels of the child. Push them alternatively so that he walks forward. Gradually, reduce the help. Start with short distances and gradually increase the distance.
2. Make the child stand with the support of a three-wheeler. Pull the three-wheeler forward slowly and let the child move forward. After the child gains confidence slowly reduce your help and let the child push.
3. Hold the child's hands and stand infront of him. While you walk backwards let the child walk forward.

Activity—14

To make the child drink by himself from a glass.

Material: A glass, a mirror and something to drink.

1. Have a small amount of liquid in a cup/glass. Show the child what he is going to drink.
2. Sit behind the child infront of mirror and physically help him to drink. When the child gains control increase the amount of liquid. Gradually reduce the help.

3. To make the child learn faster, you also drink from a glass and let the child imitate you.

Activity—15

To make the child show his body parts.

Materials: A mirror, a doll, pictures.

1. Name a part of the child's body while pointing to it. Ask the child to show it after you do. If the child speaks, let him also say the name of that part. Otherwise, let him show that part of the body, which you say. Gradually introduce the names of the other parts of the body also.
2. Let him point to the parts of the body on the doll like the doll's legs, the doll's hand and the doll's head. Later let him show the doll's nose, doll's eyes, the doll's ears etc. if he needs help, place his finger on that part which you want him to show and later let him try by himself.
3. Let him stand in front of a mirror. Make him touch his head/nose on his reflection. Whenever necessary give help to touch that part and then let him try.

Activity—16

To make the child greet others when reminded.

1. Every morning when the child wakes up and every night when the child goes to bed greet him. Insist on the child greeting you back.
2. When there are visitor in the house, have the child with you when you greet the visitor. Have the child greet the visitor.
3. Always appreciate the child for greeting appropriately.

Activity—17

To make the child jump with both feet together.

1. Hold both hands of the child and jump. Ask the child to imitate you.

2. Draw circles of one foot radius on the floor adjacent to each other, you jump from one circle to the other with both feet. Ask the child to imitate you.

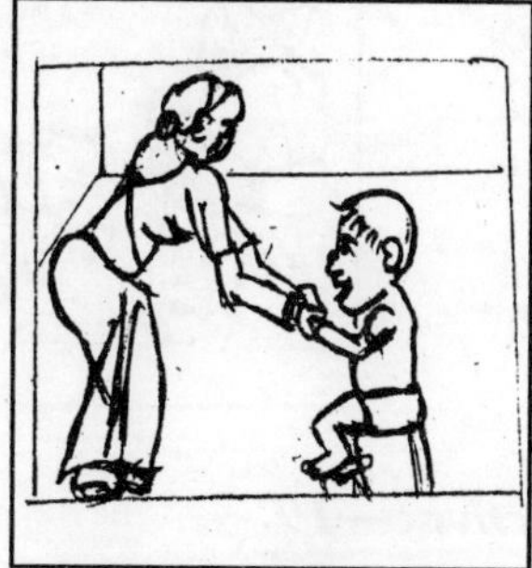

Activity—18

The make the child give verbal answers to simple questions.

Materials : Action pictures, variety of toys.

1. While the child is eating keep talking to him (now you will eat dosai and then vegetables) and in between ask him simple questions like what are you eating now, or what is in your hand? Let him answer. If he fails, let his sister, brother or a peer answer and let him imitate/repeat the answer.
2. Show him big action pictures and ask the child what the person in the picture is doing. Help him to give the answer. Gradually reduce the help.
3. Make a statement like 'I want to buy a sweet'. Ask the child' what do you want to do? Let the child say' buy a sweet'. Gradually reduce the help.
4. Keep a lot of toys and pickup one toy. Ask the child, what did I pickup?' If the child says correctly reward him. Pickup another toy and ask the child the same question. Now let him answer. Make it a game. Let him ask questions and let somebody else answer. Later let him answer somebody else's questions. Make it a point to maintain conversation with the child.

Activity—19

To make the child hold a pencil properly.

Materials: A pencil, splints, tape, rubber bands.

1. Place the pencil in the correct position in the child's hand. Make sure he rests his wrist on the writing surface. If he does not rest his wrist, place a small splint from wrist to elbow on the inner side of his fore arm and tie it loosely at the wrist and upper part of his forearm.
2. Hold the child's hands and guide him to scribble.
3. To help the child to hold appropriately a rubber band may be fixed one inch above the tip of the pencil.

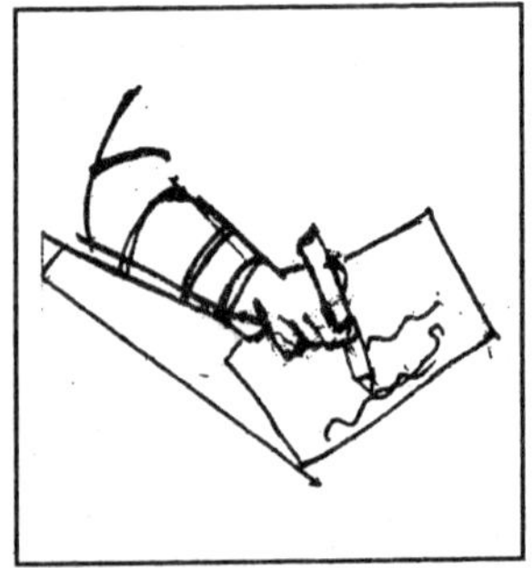

Activity—20

To make the child indicate his toilet needs.

1. Before starting the training, note and record each time he urinates or has bowel movements for at least one week. Using this record as reference, take him to the toilet 3 to 5 minutes before the noted time. Use one word always. (like : Sussu) whenever he is made to sit in the toilet.
2. Reward whenever he uses the toilet.
3. In the rural areas toilets may not be present and open ground may be used as toilets. In such instances take the child to a fixed place to make him urinate or ease himself.

Activity—21

To make the child tell his name.

1. Give the child one name and always call him with that name whenever possible.
2. Stand infront of a mirror with the child. Point at the child in the mirror and ask him, who is this? Say his name and let him repeat it.
3. Say "My name is .... and your name is ....'. Let the child say 'My name is .... (Prompt his name if necessary). Withdraw total help and give clues by whispering his name, saying the first syllable or making lip movements suggesting his name.

Activity—22

To make the child speak in small sentences.

Materials: Pictures of a story in sequence, action pictures.

1. Tell the child a story with pictures. Arrange the pictures in a sequence and ask him to narrate the story in small sentences.
2. Show him a picture poster. Ask the child to describe the actions in the poster in simple sentences.
3. Act out a simple action such as eating. Let the child say in words what he/she has seen.

Activity—23

To make the child match colours.

Materials: Beads, chips and objects of different colours.

1. Mix objects of two colours, e.g. red and green. Objects can be coloured chips, beads or cardboard cut-outs. Take out a red one and keep it separately. Take another red object and keep it with the first one as the child watches you. Now tell him to take out all the red ones and keep them with the red objects you had separated. Each time say 'red' as the child separates them.
2. Add other colours when the child is able to separate and match two colours.

Activity—24

To make the child brush his teeth.

Materials: Tooth powder, mirror, a bucket of water, a mug.

1. Brush your teeth at the same time when you want the child brush.
2. Show him how you brush and let him imitate.
3. Have a mirror in front and let the child see him while brushing.
4. If needed, initially guide him physically and gradually reduce the help and give only verbal directions. When he masters the skill reduce the direction also.

Activity—25

To make the child unbutton his clothes.

Materials: Clothing with buttons and appropriate holes, a doll.

1. Make the child unbutton by holding his hands. Then partially push the button out of the hole and let the child push it out completely.
2. Wrap his favourite toy in a cloth and button it. Ask him to unbutton the packet and take his toy. Initially, assist him and gradually let him do it himself.
3. Let the child take a doll for sand play and after the play tell that both the child and the doll are dirty and that they must bathe. Tell the child to undress the doll, so that it is ready for a bath. Help the child if necessary.

Activity—26

To make the child point to common objects by their use.

Materials: Balls, spoons, classes, pictures of familiar objects.

1. Place familiar objects such as a spoon, a ball, a doll, a glass etc., in front of the child. Show and name the item and ask the child to point to it. Praise the child when he does it.

2. Paste pictures of some items on a sheet of paper. Name and ask the child to point to them one by one. Correct the errors and appreciate the correct response.

Activity—27

To make the child walk up and down the stairs on alternate feet.

1. Stand behind the child and place his feet on your feet. Hold him at the shoulder and walk up and down the stairs. Keep talking to him on what is being done. For eg. "Let us lift one leg and put it on the lower step. Now let us lift the other leg and put it on the next step" and so on.
2. Let him hold the railing with one hand and you hold the other hand and verbally direct him to place his legs alternately on the steps. First teach him climbing up the stairs and then climbing down the stairs. Now let him hold the railing. Climb beside him without holding his hand, and finally let him climb up or down independently.

Activity—28

To make the child eat by himself.

Materials: Plate, idli, chapatti, dosa and such items.

1. Start the training with solid food items such as idli, dosa, chapatti and so on. Put a few small pieces of food in a plate and physically guide the child to pick up a piece and eat it. Gradually reduce the physical help to verbal instructions.
2. When he masters eating on his own, introduce food items such as rice, and dhal. Initially keep small balls of the food in the plate and let the child pickup a piece and eat it. Vegetable pieces should be prepared in size big enough to be picked up by the child and eaten.

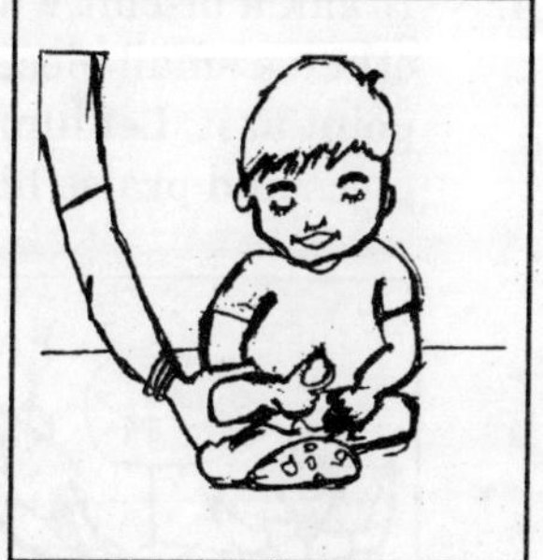

Activity—29

To make the child differentiate big and small objects

Materials: Tins or Cans of different sizes, biscuits.

1. Sort out objects according to the size. Show him two objects with a lot of difference in size. Point to the bigger one and say, this is big'. Repeat this with the smaller one.
2. Point to the child and say he is small. Point to yourself and say you are big. Use appropriate gestures to say big and small.
3. Draw two circles, one big and the other small. Ask him to stand in the small circle. Point to the small circles and let him stand in it.
4. Break a biscuit with two parts, one big piece and the other, a small piece. Ask him to take the big piece and point at it. Let him say "big". Give him the big biscuit piece and praise him.

Activity—30

To make the child copy patterns.

Materials: paper, a pencil.

1. Draw a pattern that has to be copied. Hold the child's hand and physically guide him to trace the pattern. After a few trails let the child draw on the line on his own. Assist him if needed.

2. Draw the pattern with dotted lines. Help the child to join the dots.
3. Draw the pattern and ask the child to copy it.

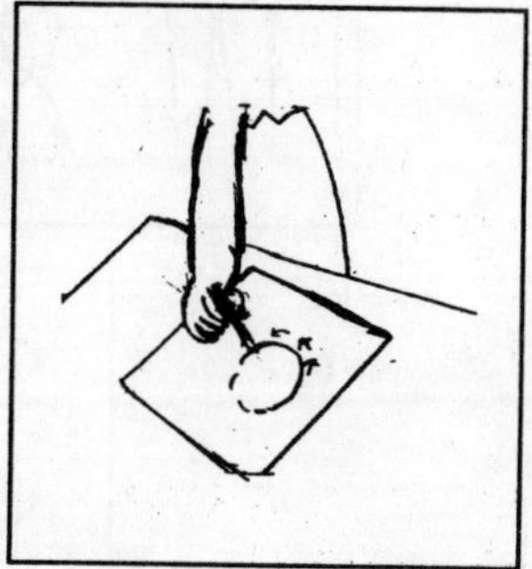

Activity—31

To make the child button his clothes.

Materials: Clothing with large buttons.

1. Button your shirt/coat as the child watches. Help him to do likewise by giving him attractive coat/shirt with big buttons.
2. Push the button half way through and let him complete by pushing it through the buttonhole and pulling it out with the other hand.
3. Stand behind the child. Hold his hands and make him button his shirt. Gradually reduce the assistance and let him do it independently.
4. Give verbal directions and let him button the shirt. Start with large buttons and slowly reduce the size of the buttons.

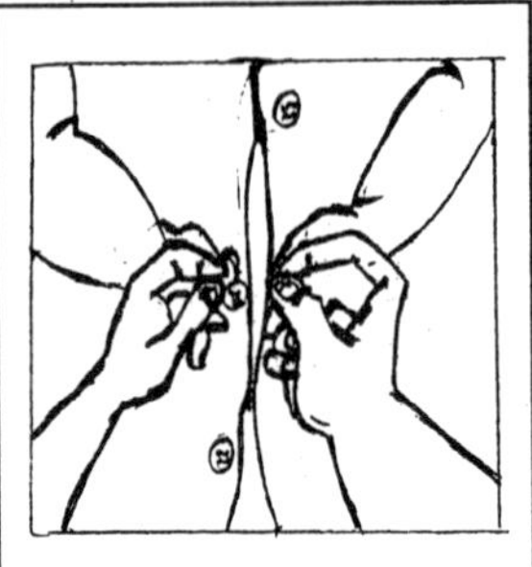
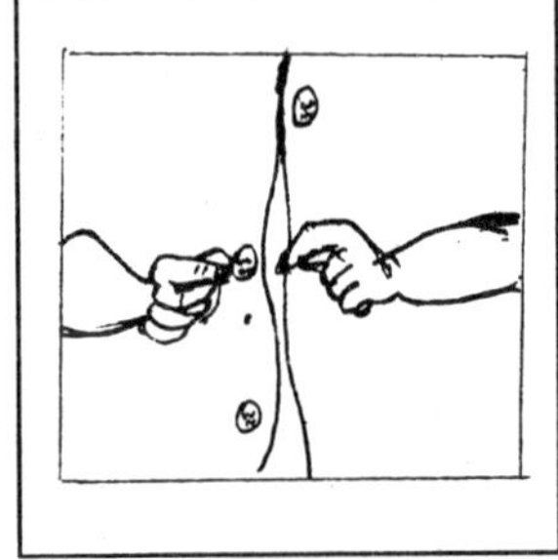

Activity—32

To make the child comb his hair

Materials: A mirror, a comb.

1. Comb your hair while the child watches. Ask him to comb your hair by giving him the comb. Comb your hair and ask him to imitate.
2. Make him stand in front of a mirror and let him try combing. If necessary, help him to comb his hair. Gradually reduce your help. Let him do independently.

Activity—33

To make the child wash his face.

Materials: A tub with water, a mug, a soap, a towel.

1. Instruct the child to bend at his hip/squat splash water over the face from a vessel. Help him to apply soap on his hands. Tell him to close his eyes and apply soap on the face.
2. Give him the vessel with water and ask him to splash on his face. Initially help him and gradually reduce the help. Give him the towel to wipe is face.

Activity—34

To make the child associate the time of the day with activity

Materials: Pictures of various activities.

1. Associate the day with the Sun and the night with the Moon. Show that the lights are switched on during the nighttime.
2. Talk to the child about the activities done during various time of the day such as eating breakfast in the morning, lunch in the afternoon, playing in the evening and sleeping in the night.
3. When the child goes to bed tell him that when he wakes up it will be morning.
4. Pictures of various activities can be used to say which time of the day the activity takes place.

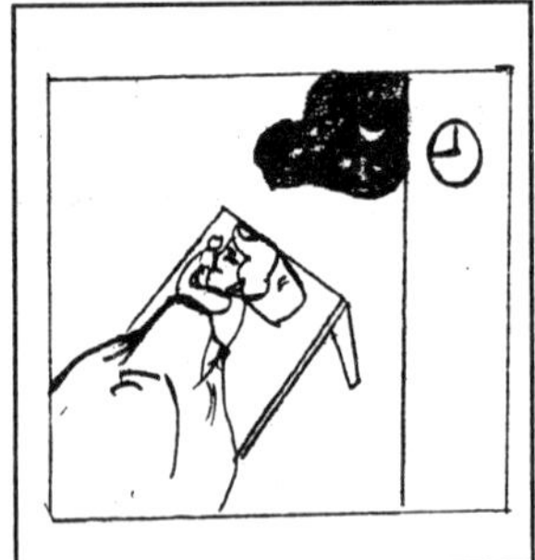

Activity—35

To make the child count up to 10 by rote.

Materials: Ten objects

1. Say the numbers from one to ten and make the child repeat one by one.

2. Make a row of ten objects and make the child count after you do.
3. Let him walk up or down the stairs and count each step.

Activity—36

To make the child name the colours of the objects when shown.

Materials: Bangles, toys, clothing.

1. After the child sorts out the colours, point to one colour and ask him what it is. If he cannot say, name the colour. To make the child name 'red', show him the things in red such as tomatoes, apple, red in coloured clothing, bangles, bindi and so on. Let him say the colour of those items.
2. Similarly, teach the other colours and associate them to things in everyday living. Such things need not be taught during training sessions only but can be taught at any time of the day under any circumstances.

Activity—37

To make the child follow two unrelated instructions.

1. Give the child are instruction such as 'close the door'. When he is able to do that, give two instructions such as 'open the window and get the plate'. If the does only one, ask him what the other instruction was. If he fails to say or remember prompt him. Do not give complicated commands during the initial stages.

Activity—38

To make the child name the days of the week,

1. Say the names of the week and let the child repeat one by one.
2. Make a rhythm of the days of the week and teach it as a song to the child.
3. Every morning ell him what day it is and what day would follow. If possible make him change the day and date in the calendar.

Activity—39

To make the child read simple words.

Materials: Pictures of familiar objects with written/printed names

1. Show him pictures of common animals, objects of everyday use, etc. and various modes of transport etc. and name them. When he recognises the pictures add the written name. Expose the picture written with the word many times. When you are sure the child knows it well, separate the word from the picture. Remember to show only two pictures with the names at a time. When the child is able to match correctly give the word alone without the picture and let him read it. Later, as and when the word is seen at any places ask the child to read it.
2. Always begin with simple, two letter words. Later, words which we come across in day to day life such as men, women, danger, poison, etc. can be taught.

Activity—40

To make the child count meaningfully upto ten.

1. Use beads, stones, bottle caps or such others small items. Have two small cups, drop one stone in each cup saying one. In the same way drop, two, three and so on.
2. Let the child repeat what you did. Correct him if he drops more or less number of stones.
3. Ask the child to give you a desired amount. If he gives you incorrectly, correct him. Start with small numbers and then proceed to bigger ones.
4. Generalize the activity by asking him to count the number of people in room, number of trees, number of windows in the room and so on.

Summary

Early identification and assessment form a foundation for developing early intervention programme. Early identification helps a teacher to identify the abilities and disabilities. Identification and assessment of mentally retarded children includes evaluating general intelligence and adaptive behaviour. Various standardised tests are available to assess general intelligence, adaptive behaviour and specific abilities. In addition to diagnostic testing, psychological testing also goes in hand in early identification. Once the mental age of a child is assessed, early intervention programme can be framed depending upon the child performance ability. Long-term objectives and short-term goals help to proceed to the child's progress. Short-term goals should be further divided into sub tasks/activities and task analysis is to be carried out. Task analysis is the process of breaking down the task into small sequential steps. These simple sequential tasks were trained with reinforcement. The follow-up and periodic record keeping is major imperatives for successful and effective early intervention programmes.

4

Educational Programmes for Mentally Retarded Children

OBJECTIVES

In this chapter, the authors delineated the educational services, educational programmes and instructional strategies for educating mentally retarded. After reading this chapter the readers are able to:

1. Know the educational placements services available for mentally retarded children;
2. Know the educational programmes for mentally retarded children;
3. Know and develop skills in planning and development of various instructional strategies to teach mentally retarded children;
4. Know and understand the ways and means of behaviour modification.

Introduction

There are so many works, books and periodicals on care, training, educational and treatment of mentally retarded children. Eventhough there are so many guidelines, there is no clarity in remediating the problems of mentally retarded children. At this juncture, it is an attempt to give a clear picture about how to train and educate mentally retarded to make them as independent as possible. Once if we know the concept, meaning, definition and ways of identification and assessment, it is easy to categorize the mentally retarded children based on their IQ and current level of performance. Once they are classified in a group, educational plan can be drawn. This classification is very useful for educational purpose. Each group has its unique characteristics and problems requiring a distinct and unique kind of educational programmes. Hence, appropriate placement procedure should be carried out to provide effective educational programmes.

Educational Provisions for Mentally Retarded

There are various educational programmes available for mentally retarded children. They are: Regular classroom, Special class, Special school, Home based instruction, Custodial care or Hospital services and Residential institutions. In the process of selecting educational delivery options it is important to keep in mind that;

(i) educational placement should be based on the child's needs,

(ii) the child should be places in the most facilitate or least restrictive environment, and

(iii) placement should be flexible enough that a child could be moved to a different settings if the situation warrants it.

Placement process is an important task that has to be carried out based on the child's ability. Proper care should be given to select appropriate placement services based on the child's needs. To place these children in the least restrictive environment there are several placement services. They are:

(i) Regular Classroom

Educable mentally retarded children are usually benefit from regular classroom placement then trainable mentally retarded children. They require some support services from itinerant teachers who visit the schools and work with the child on a part time basis. Consulting service for the regular classroom teacher to handle these children effectively is also provided by itinerant teacher helps educable mentally retarded to be successful in the regular classroom. Part-time attendance in a separate resource room staffed by a special education teacher, gives extra help in a basic subject such as reading or mathematics.

Children with lower intellectual and adaptive behaviour levels require more special services. They also present problems in the regular classroom. Individual instructional plan and behaviour modification programme should be drafted for such children to make them progress and to integrate them with their peers.

(ii) Special Class

Children those who have academic and adaptive behaviour problems preclude placement in the regular classroom should be placed in special class. There are two special class options namely part time placement and full-time placement. Educable mentally retarded children with severe academic problems may be placed in special class. The children with good adaptive behaviour remain in the special class for academic work and effective by mingle with classmates for physical education, art, music, and other activities in which academic skills are not crucial. Children who are in need for intensive instruction in academic area and adaptive behaviour may be placed in full-time placement in a special class.

Some trainable mentally retarded children and severe/profound mentally retarded will be educated in full-time, self-contained special classes. The stress is on self-help skills, basic communication skills and vocational skill development. Such education and training helps the child to be employed in a supervised or sheltered job site. School personnel should try to foster effective social interactions that help them to interact with non-handicapped children successfully.

(iii) Special School

In India too, special schools are slowly disappearing because of mainstreaming. In the past, it was common practice to house all education programmes for handicapped children in special schools. This placement service is appropriate only for children who cannot profit from integration in regular schools. These children suffer from severe academic problems and adaptive behaviour. They are in need of individual attention and training in daily living skills. These individuals' needs are effectively met in special school placement services.

(iv) Home based Instruction

Home based programme is generally provided only to those who cannot attend school because of a medical or physical problem, when a child required complete bed care. Some mentally retarded children cannot attend and profit from school and such children can be provided with home based instruction. Most home based instruction is short-term and provided only while the child is recovering from a temporary, illness or disorder.

(v) Custodial Care or Hospital Care and Residentia Institutions

Mentally retarded children who are unable to profit fr the above said placement services and have severe problems are placed in custodial care. Severe/profoundly mentally retarded children are found more frequently in this settings. The children who are in need of support even to perform daily living skills are placed in residential institutions. Caretaker should be there to look after their needs.

There are some of the educational provisions for the mentally retarded children. Based on the child's ability, performance level and child's need, educational services are to be provided. Appropriate services helps them to progress at their own pace.

Education for Educable Mentally Retarded Children

Educable mentally retarded (EMR) children are those who are not able to be adequately educated in the regular classroom. However, they can acquire sufficient knowledge and ability in the academic areas that are useful to function effectively in later life. They will be able to receive basic academic skills (reading, writing and arithmetic) and acquire self-help skill, which supports them to be socially and economically independent. So the objectives of an educational programme for the educable group are, in general, the same as the educational objectives for all children. They should be educated to make the greatest use of their abilities to satisfy their own needs as well as the demands of the society in which they are living. The objective of an educational programme should centre upon three specific objectives namely:

1. personal or emotional adjustment;
2. social adjustment; and
3. economic adjustment.

Objectives of the programme are achieved only if the organization of the programme, methods of instruction, selection and use of materials for instruction are effective. For this, teachers should be thoroughly trained to work with mentally retarded children. They should have a sound background in the education of normal children and in child growth and development. While providing education curriculum for the primary class should include 1) mental and physical health, 2) social experiences, 3) readiness activities, 4) quantitative concepts, 5) motor skills and 6) experience with simple tools and common materials. During elementary level, mentally retarded children should be given training in basic living skills and on academic skills to provide proficiency in their use. Secondary school curriculum should centre on 1) the consolidation of social and academic skills, 2) expanded application of academic skills and introduction to jobs and job requirements. Higher secondary school curriculum should concentrate on extension of social experiences and general occupational information and 2) correlated work-school experiences to prepare the mentally retarded youth for the world of work. The above stated curriculum should be imparted with highly organized and sequenced instructional methods. The teacher should carry out instruction in slow rate than for normal children. Variety of experiences and opportunities should be given to the child to learn and exhibit the target skills. Educable mentally retarded individual can be trained with basic academic skills. They can understand and benefit upto sixth grade level. They can also be trained to perform daily living skills independently. They are also be made economically and socially independent as much as possible by giving vocational education. Educable mentally retarded children can be trained to work in the sheltered workshops and in open employment. There will be a supervisor in sheltered workshops to monitor them and able to direct to work better. Such work experiences inturn will facilitate to enter in the open society for their better survival.

Educational Programme for Trainable Mentally Retarded

Trainable mentally retarded children have little or no readiness for academic subjects and so they never develop usable skills in 3 R's (reading, writing and arithmetic). So they need a different manner of training than that of educable mentally retarded individual. Training should help them to live happily and safely in his or her social environment. The objective of the training programme should concentrate on 1) self-care, 2) social adjustment, 3) work habits and skills, 4) speech and language development, and 5) diversional activities. The training programme will vary from child to child according to their potential and developmental level of the child. Concrete, meaningful and stimulating activities and experiences should be used while giving training to trainable mentally retarded children. All the children within a class will not be ready to learn the same activity at the same time. They will not progress at equal rate. After thorough diagnosis and classification according to the ability and current performance level, the teacher should design Individualised Educational Plan (IEP). Trainable mentally retarded individuals have extremely very limited mental ability and most of their IEP is non-academic in nature.

Training should not be confined within the classroom. Continuity of training at home or in the ward/hospital should be ensured through the parents or attendant. Even then, education of mentally retarded children should be carried out in the following areas:

1. Language development
2. Motor development
3. Social development
4. Physical health
5. Daily living skills
6. Recreational and creative expression skill training
7. Yoga therapy and
8. Work habits and skills.

1. Language Development

Language development programmes for mentally retarded can be conducted in classroom and at home with the help of teachers and parents. To improve speech and language, group participation will help an individual. Language development programmes will help to demonstrate and exercise auditory and visual discrimination. Mentally retarded child will not differ in speech development than the normal child except that the processes are slower to develop. Speech, like many other learned activities, is grasped through example and imitation. Repetition method will help the child in language acquisition. It should be incorporated into the daily routine of the home. Study while planning technique should be followed by the teachers as well as by the parents. When the child is playing with toys, identify them, use them and explain their function. At meal times, names of different food items, eating utensils, a discussion and conversation at the dining table with other family members helps to acquire speech and language.

Various types of simple, concrete pictures of foods, clothing, furniture and other similar objects within the child's immediate environment can also be used for vocabulary building, articulation and sentence formulation. Different types of activities such as whistles, horns and other noisemaking devices as well as candles, balloons and other blowing material which helps in dealing with problems of breathing and breath control, palatal movement and similar difficulties also help in language acquisition.

Speech therapy should be given to the mentally retarded children by speech therapist. Eventhough speech training is carried out by the therapist, parent's also play an important role in speech training.

2. Motor Development

In motor development fine motor co-ordination and gross motor co-ordination have to be developed. Mentally retarded individual exhibit very poor motor co-ordination in both fine motor and gross motor activities. Training programme for mentally retarded children should cover the motor development. Activities that call for large movements of muscles such as—throwing a ball, skipping the rope, using an axe, hammer helps in development of gross motor co-ordination. Fine motor co-ordination activities such as-picking up small objects, counting beads, threading the needle, unscrewing and screwing bolts and nuts will help the mentally retarded individual to develop fine motor co-ordination. This activities will inturn develop muscular control and co-ordination. Physiotherapy and occupational therapy is also very useful in the motor development. Therapies should be carried out by the trained therapists. Parents also play an important role in the training of motor activities. They have to carryout the therapy in the home as directed by the therapist. All these activities must be adjusted to the capabilities of the child grouping of the children with approximately the same degree of ability provides stimulus or inactive for progress.

3. Social Development

Social development begins with good social contact and relationships with elders. Social adjustment is achieved through social interaction rather than through formal teaching. Teachers' and parents must structure and organize students' environment so that they are provided with maximum opportunity to develop social adjustment. They are trained at a high level of moral reasoning and also exhibit pro-social behaviour towards others. Various intervention strategies and techniques are used to develop positive feelings and internal control over their behaviour.

Good manners, consideration of others, respect for authority and a degree of responsibility are some of the areas that have to be included to make the mentally retarded children to be socially adjusted.

4. Health and Safety Skills

While training mentally retarded children activities related to health habits and safety skills should have a place in it, because health and safety skills helps mentally retarded individual to achieve social maturity. If a mentally retarded child is well trained with good health habits, personal grooming and good social habits it will help to make the child more acceptable to others. As the children learns to participate, to share, to co-operate and to take turns in activities he/she acquires greater social maturity and helps them to live more acceptable form by others.

5. Daily Living Skills

Personal grooming activities like how to eat, how to dress and undress, caring teeth, face, hair, nails, toilet training and to take care of his clothing, appearance and personal belonging should find place in training programmes.

Toilet training is more important among personal grooming activities. They should be trained when and where to go to the toilet, proper use of bowls, and toilet tissue, washing hands, and adjusting clothing.

Mentally retarded children should also be made aware of physical hazards and external hazards. Physical hazards such as—pushing and shouting, biting, throwing and hitting, kicking and tripping, using sharp instruments and handling extremely hot and cold materials are to be known by the mentally retarded children. They also needs training how to avoid the above said physical hazards.

Hazards caused from situations arising with traffic, animals, plants and during play time activities is also made known to the mentally retarded children by providing training in developing safety habits which are applicable in all contexts among mentally retarded children.

6. Recreational and Creative Expression Skill Training

The diversional or recreational activities release the child from routine. These activities should be designed so as to stimulate the imagination and to develop some creative thinking. These activities help the child to live with others. The idea of sharing can also be incorporated in this area as well as the arts, crafts, physical activity and recreation, music and nature studies. They can be engaged with a variety of activities like clay or wood modelling, plaster of paris, soap carving, puppetry, sculpturing, metal work, plastics, drawing, block building etc. The choice of activities should be made by the teachers carefully based on the child's ability and current performance level.

7. Yoga Therapy

Yoga and meditation can also be carried out while giving training programme for the mentally retarded children. Yoga and exercise will help the children to improve concentration and memory level. They also get muscular co-ordination. Yoga therapy also makes them to relax and improve self-confidence among mentally retarded children. Only the personnel should conduct yoga class and giving training to the parents can carry it out at home. Yoga finds an important place while developing training programme for the mentally retarded children.

8. Work Habits and Skills

Work habits and skills help mentally retarded children to be vocationally rehabilitated. Developing work habits and skills even at the younger stage will help to develop readiness skills which are important to become economically independent in later life.

The planned curriculum is effectively imparted with the use of best intervention strategies and instructional methods. Training in cover making, packing work, craft work, book binding, agarbathi making, candle making and other works will give economic independence and can be imparted in the vocational curriculum both for educable and trainable mentally retarded children.

Education for Profound/Severe Mentally Retarded Children

Academic aspects can't come into the framework of educational programmes for the profound/severely mentally retarded children. Apart from academic aspects very basic self-help skills can be taught. Educational programmes for profound/ severely retarded children should have the following features such as:

- — Age appropriate curriculum and materials
- — Functional activities
- — Community based instruction
- — Integrated therapy
- — Integration with on-retarded peers
- — Family involvement.

According to the child's ability level and mental age, appropriate curriculum has to be designed. The focus of educational programmes should be more flexible and practical. The designed activities will be more effective if it is carried out in the community. Many severe/profound mentally retarded individuals have multiple disabilities that warrants the services of a variety of professionals such as speech, physical and occupational therapists. This type of children will benefit better with the integrated therapy. Interaction with non-retarded peers facilitates for better understanding and leads to normalisation or socialisation of retarded students. The most important for the success of educational programmes for the severe/profound mentally retarded children is family involvement. As many of the cases are of bedridden and are not in a position to be placed in an institution, home based training programme instruction is given in the home bound situation. So while educating profound mentally retarded children special teachers should possess patience, sincerity and tolerance to deal this type of children. The prime aim of special education is to make the mentally retarded children to be socially and economically independent. But for this category, only training in some basic self-help skills should be the aim of special education.

Instructional Methods and Strategies in Teaching Mentally Retarded

Teaching and learning is a process of interaction between teacher and student. This interaction facilitates students to use strategies to actively construct their mental structures. Strategy teaching plays a vital role in the construction of students' mental structures. Bill R. Gearheart et al. (1988) listed out five basic rules for the teachers in strategy teaching. They are:

1. make strategies clear and explicit;
2. build new strategies on old strategies;
3. apply strategies directly to task;
4. emphasize transfer and generalisation; and
5. emphasize self regulation through strategy use.

The above authors also explained three approaches to teaching strategies: the Tell them method, the Model-it method, and the Develop-it method. They can be used separately or in combination.

(i) Tell-them Method

Telling students about a strategy has the advantage of requiring less time than the other two methods. Also some students may lack the knowledge or skill that are required for developing strategy with the teacher. One disadvantage of this method is that self regulated thinking may not occur. Second disadvantage over this method is that it has to little emphasis on the current thinking of the student about the task. So while using tell-them method teacher required careful, detailed planning of the exact steps in the strategy.

Specific steps for teachers to follow with the tell-them method are:

1. Analyse current thinking and performance of the students;
2. Generate disequilibrium. Be sure students know the old strategy is adequate;
3. State the steps in the strategy. Tell them what they need to know to use the strategy;

4. Tell them how to use the strategy;
5. Require practice with the strategy;
6. Require transfer to other tasks and settings;
7. Follow-up to assure strategy use.

(ii) Model-it Method

This method requires more than just telling students about a strategy. This is nothing but direct demonstrations of a method to the learners. This method can be used as a sub step in tell-them method or in develop-it method. This method is more efficient than the develop-it method, but may take more time than tell-them method.

The model-it method is explained by Finch and Spirito (1980), Meichenbaum (1977), and others who emphasize the use of cognitive behaviour modification. Research by these writers indicates that some individuals can learn to modify their behaviour by using verbal self-instruction. The steps in the method as presented by Meichenbaum are:

1. *Cognitive modelling:* The model (teacher) performs the task while talking out loud about how he or she is thinking, as the student observes.
2. *Overt guidance:* The student performs the task under the teachers guidance, instructing himself or herself by talking out loud in imitation of the teacher.
3. *Overt self-guidance:* The student performs the task without teacher guidance instructing himself or herself by talking out loud.
4. *Faded overt self-guidance:* The student performs the task while whispering the instructions.
5. *Covert Self-guidance:* The student performs the task using private speech (" saying the instructions in his or her head).

Teacher and student use four general types of verbalisations. They are:

1. problem-definition statements;

2. focus attention and provide response guidance;
3. self-evaluation, error correcting or coping; and
4. self-reinforcement statements.

Model-it method appears useful for learning new strategies, for using strategies that are already known, and for transferring strategies to appropriate settings.

(iii) Develop-it Method

Develop-it method uses a dialogue between the teacher and the student to create a strategy. In this method the teacher guides dialogue carefully so that an effective strategy is devised cooperatively. More than one strategy is suggested during the discussion. Alternative strategies can also be tried out and modified and the most effective one is selected. Develop-it method can be used with a single student or with a group. This method has direct student involvement. It helps students for their own learning. The method is also very time consuming. The main advantage of this method is developing a strategy by themselves may be more effective than having a strategy imposed on them.

The above discussed three approaches provide a means for the teacher to interact with the student in a productive way. The teacher's task is to understand the learner, the nature of learning and the curriculum and then to use methods that enable learners to construct their own version of reality, flexible, integrated use of the three approaches is essential.

Certain Strategies used in Educating Mentally Retarded

Strategies are of two types: student strategies and teacher strategies. Teachers help students to develop strategies and improve them. They enable the students to guide their own thinking and behaviour. In cueing strategies an individual can learn to use to guide thinking and behaviour. Cueing strategies are of two types. They are: perceptual cueing strategies and language cueing strategies. Perceptual cueing strategies are presenting visual signs or symbols to remind students to use a strategy or the steps in a strategy. Language cueing strategies use verbal and written language cues to accomplish the same purpose. Bill R. Gearheart et al. (1988) described the following strategies in their book 'Teaching Mildly and Moderately Handicapped Students'. Their strategies explained here would be useful in teaching, mild, moderately and severely retarded children. They are:

(i) Perceptual cueing strategies

(ii) Language cueing strategies

(iii) Reading strategies

(iv) Written language strategies

(v) Strategies in mathematics

(i) Perceptual Cueing Strategies

Perceptual cueing strategies typically involve presenting visual signs or symbols to the steps in a strategy (DeRuiter and Wansart, 1982). Language cueing strategies use verbal and written language cues to accomplish the same purposes. Handicapped students need to use cueing strategies in the way they must be active participants in learning. Strategies are presented in five categories namely—attention, perception, motor performance, memory and comprehension.

Cueing for Attention: DeRuiter and Wansart (1982) explain that students who are hyperactive will fail to focus on the important stimuli that will help them to accomplish a task. Hyperactive children have problems in organising and planning to do a task. When attention getting visual cues is used for this type of children they perform better (Sykes et al. 1973). Increasing size of the stimuli, adding colours, additional visual markers, (i.e., arrows or pointers) and underlining are some of the attention drawing strategies.

Cueing for Perception: This cueing is similar to cueing for attention, but emphasis should be on discriminating ability between stimuli than by simply attending to them. Clear examples, contrast in the stimulus, redundant cues, and cues in increased size may certainly develop discrimination learning. This will facilitate the students to develop and use their own cueing strategies to aid perception in a wide variety of tasks.

Motor Performance Cueing: Motor performance can be developed by two kinds of visual cues. They are: modelling and illustrations.

Model: Model the performance directly so that the student can imitate the movements. Zane, Walls, and Thevedt (1981) researched the best way to teach moderately and severely retarded adults to assemble complex objects. Whole-task modelling before the subjects did the task was more successful than such techniques as providing one-word prompts-"good" or "no" or allowing the subjects to make errors and then correcting them.

Illustrations: Illustrations or visual cues may serve better for some students. Hayes (1982) found that visual cues, when combined with verbal cues and subject verbalisation, were helpful to kindergarten and third grade students in learning to reproduce letter-like forms. But certainly students learn most motor performance activities by practising the movement directly.

Memory: Young children are able to use visual cues to aid memory and recall. Visual imagery is an aid in using perceptual cues to promote memory. Visual imagery can be used effectively with people of different ages and with a variety of tasks (Higbee, 1976). Klatzky (1975) defines a mnemonic device, as "a rule system of rule or that has been developed to improve our ability to recall items". There are two types of mnemonics. They are: organising mnemonics and encoding mnemonics. Bellezza (1981) suggested these types.

Organising Mnemonics: Organising mnemonics are techniques for associating or relating items that at first appear unrelated so that they can be remembered. Story mnemonics also helps to remember and recall better. Encoding operations is nothing but including concrete word encoding by involving visual object abstractly based on meaning or semantically, by picturing an object that has a similar meaning. Phonetic encoding is association based on sound similarities. Forrest (1981) suggests a strategy in which students picture themselves in action.

Another visual mnemonic technique is called keyword. Atkinson (1975) developed this technique for learning second languages and has been applied and tested by Jones and Hall (1982) Levin and his colleagues (1981), Levin et al. (1982) and Shriberg et al. (1982). Keyword mnemonics "involve physically transforming to-be-learned materials into a form that makes them easier to learn and remember" (Levin, 1981).

Comprehension: Perceptual cues that help the learner to select understand and remember ideas. Cueing for comprehension involves three strategies—underlining, mapping and picture symbols. Glover et al. (1980) and Schnell and Rocchio (1974) tested underlining strategies among college students and high school students. In both studies, underlining was used in reading comprehension tasks, and ways to teach effective underlining were examined. Glover et al. concludes that college students were able to organise and remember material better after they received training in how to underline. These students also transferred this strategy to standardised comprehension tests. In Schnell and Rocchio study, high school students found that underlining could result in improvement in comprehension.

Mapping is the next perceptual cueing strategies (Driskell, 1977) or brain patterns (Buzan, 1976). According to Buzan this technique encourages the use of holistic, associative patterns that are natural top human thinking.

Picture symbols: This is a strategy for associating a perceptual cue with each step in another strategy the student is using. Shape symbol strategy can be used as a additional reminder. Students are first presented with symbols that are not associated with the specific label for the step could be used. Next, the pictures are placed on a card with the associated words removed. Strategies like this will take some time to develop and may provide more structure that some students need.

Overall, each of the above discussed strategies may be useful cues. A teacher who is dealing mild, moderately and severely handicapped students may have to use auditory, tactile or other sensory cues if such cues appear beneficial to their students.

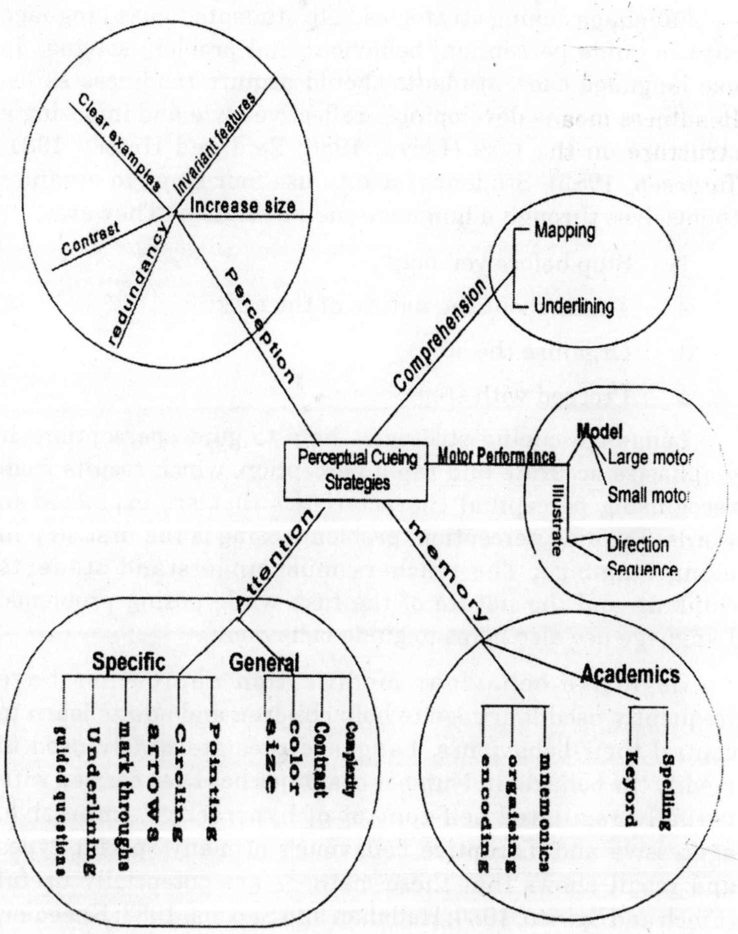

A Map of Perceptual Cueing Strategies

(ii) Language Cueing Strategies

Language cueing strategies help students to use language cues to guide perception, behaviour and problem solving. To use language cues, students should acquire readiness skills. Readiness means developing a reflective style and imposing a structure on the task (Lloyd, 1980; Reid and Hresko 1981; Torgesen, 1982). Students have to use four steps to organise themselves through a language cueing strategy. They are:

1. Stop before you act;
2. Think about the nature of the task;
3. Organise the steps;
4. Proceed with steps.

Language cueing strategies help to guide perception. It emphasise accurate and rapid perception, which results from recognising perceptual characteristics that are explained in words. To guide perception, problem posing is the first step in using language. The teachers must understand students thinking and the nature of the task while posing problems. Language use also helps to guide behaviour.

Cognitive behaviour modification approaches have frequently used language to help children and adults learn to control their behaviours. Language cues are widely used to modify the behaviour. Number of studies has been carried with verbally regulated self-control of hyperactive, impulsive, aggressive and disruptive behaviours of many specific types and result shows that these methods are potentially useful (Finch and Spirito, 1980; Hallahan and Sapona, 1983; Kneedler, 1980; Keogh and Glover, 1980; Meichenbaun, 1977). Three step strategy was used by Brown and Alford (1984) to study the effect of cognitive behaviour modification technique on the control of attention and academic performance. Students are told to a) stop and define the problem and the steps in it, b) consider and evaluate solutions before acting on any one and c) verbalise the strategy throughout the training. The subjects were taught several tasks with the emphasis on this strategies to pay close attention compared to a control group with similar attention disorders, the trained group was significantly higher in several means uses of attention and academic performance. Language cues are also useful in guiding problem solving. Many different tasks and learners with wide variations in abilities can be fitted within this framework. The components of the framework are (1) problem awareness, (2) organising the task, (3) learning new information, and applying a solution strategy.

The major step for problem solving is to become aware of the nature of the problem. Problem awareness focuses on discovering what the task requires. It requires careful observation. Organising the task is carried out after getting awareness about the problem. It has two sub components—representing the problem and planning a solution (Hayes, 1981).

Posed problems are solved with two main approaches: Open search and Closed search. When problem solver is uncertain about to plan a solution open search is used. When a solution plan is not known, the problem solver tries out possible strategies based on what is known about the problem and modifies the strategy if it is unsuccessful. Self-questioning strategies may be useful (Hayes, 1981). This method is used once the students have gathered adequate information about the problem. Trial and error strategies are most useful when the problem solver is uncertain about how to proceed and the problem is relatively small. Breaking the problem helps to solve complex problems with several parts. The second approach i.e., closed search is frequently used in academic tasks because the learner already knows the strategies that are required to do the task but needs to select a strategy from among those that are known. Elaborate approaches include strategies such as self questioning with open ended questions, drawing inferences, or providing self generated examples. Once we know a problem collaborative strategies must be put into action if it to lead to solution.

In solving some problem, problem solver learns new information before a problem is solved. New learning ranges from simple to very complex. The last step in problem solving framework is to apply the solution strategy. Enable the students to regulate their own solution strategies. Thus language can be used as a mediator in three major areas—as a guide for perception, for behaviour and for problem solving.

(iii) Reading Strategies

Smith (1978) suggests that in order to learn to read, children must be totally immersed in 'print'. The environment that is encouraging, rewarding and meaningful helps the children to read better. The effective method of teaching reading is to read to the child, to read with the child, and to permit the child to read'.

To promote better reading, the selected materials must be meaningful. Meaningfulness is nothing but the reader's interest and abilities. Once meaningful material is selected for reading to the student, method is adopted who do not yet read or are just beginning. Reading with dialogue is also followed. The teacher should use her knowledge of the children's ability to understand to decide about topics for discussion, the teacher makes comments, asks probing questions, explores and encourages thinking about the story and provides opportunities for the student to ask questions and make comments. Participating in the process of learning is the import ant aspects of learning to read. In the second stage reading with students, most direct reading instruction occurs.

Specific information about words and sounds may be presented in this step. There are some of the approaches used in reading. Fernald method (Fernald, 1943) is an approach that combines language experience with multisensory procedures (Kirk, Kliebhan, and Lerner, 1978). Fernald method and Brown's modification of Fernald method place considerable emphasis on making the reading process meaningful for the students.

Letting the students to read on their own is useful to read at their own pace and purpose. In developing reading, all stages of reading should focus on constructing meanings, amount of reading takes place, dialogue about reading processes and content. In reading, comprehension strategies questioning is the major component. It involves complex processes that require considerable language and cognitive understanding.

Reading is a continuous process of constructing and reconstructing new meanings at increasingly higher levels. Thus learning to read is a natural process that will take place primarily through the act of reading itself. Teachers play a major role in learning to read. They have to provide as much reading as possible and provide interactive dialogue about the reading process and content for better reading.

(iv) Written Language Strategy

Written expression is a complex process. Written expression may be considered as a continuous and constructive process of exploration, rehearsal, drafting and revision (Daigon, 1982). This is similar with that of Piagetian conceptualisation in which individuals construct and refine their knowledge to higher levels of complexity through continuous interaction with the environment. In written expression, the writer not only writes to say but also how to say it, purpose of writing, writing style and determines the intended audience.

Written expression centres on punctuation, capitalization, spelling and handwriting—through students express their thoughts. Educational programme for mildly and moderately retarded also focuses on writing skills. It has to be developed among them in order to achieve overall rehabilitation. Written skills help an individual in daily living situations. This may be particularly true for students identified as mildly and moderately retarded children.

A strategy-based teaching and learning approach in which both teacher and student strategies are intended to help students to become more independent in their writing and more aware of the elements involved in becoming a writer. Child's current functioning level in writing should be assessed and then the intervention programme should be designed.

It is so important for children to attend to print and respond to it if they are to learn more about reading and writing. Writing is a process involving the composing of a message, the transcription of message and the evaluation of what has written. Witting is a skill consisting of three components namely: Pre-writing, writing and post-writing (Daigon, 1982; Poloway, Patton and Cohen, 1981). Each component requires careful planning and instruction for success. Pre-writing explores topic, positive and safe environment, motivate students to write. Determine the purpose of writing and determining the audience are important for better writing.

The following points are useful for teachers in organising their strategies for written language instruction. 1) Make the students to understand the purposes for writing. 2) Develop pre-writing skills among mentally retarded individual. Play way technique helps to develop pre-writing and writing skills among the mentally retarded individual. Dot joining, overwriting, copying and writing from memory are some of the activities helpful in developing readiness skill needed for writing.

Joining Dots (Patterned Outline)

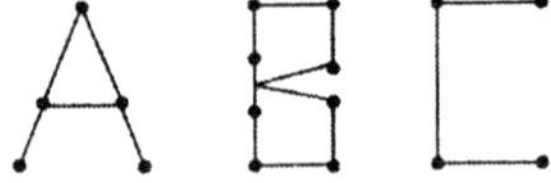

Various recreational activities like colouring, painting, drawing will also enhance writing skills. Such type of diversional activities should also be incorporated in the curriculum for teaching writing skills. The objective of the educational programme is achieved with the help of play-way learning method. Grinnel and Burris (1983) and Calkins (1979) state the use for a drawing to help the students think about what they are going to write. These authors point out that younger writers move back and forth between drawing and print as they are learning to communicate in writing. Drawing is very effective with the students who are slow starters and slow writers. While concentrating on writing skills, spelling and handwriting are the sub skills that have to be concentrated for developing good writing skill. Spelling and handwriting can be developed using various strategies. Drill and practice method helps to write letters legibly.

Modelling, physical prompts and cues, copying, self-verbalization, writing from memory, repetition, self-correction, feedback and reinforcement are some of the procedures useful in teaching letter formation.

(v) Strategies in Teaching Mathematics

Basic arithmetic skills have to be imparted among mild and moderately retarded children. This knowledge is very important to rehabilitate them both socially and economically. Arithmetic skills such as numbers, simple addition, subtraction, multiplication, division and some basic mathematical skills are very useful in daily life situations. Such skills should be taught to the mentally retarded individual. While providing educational programme for the mildly retarded children, basic arithmetic skills upto sixth grade level is appropriate. Activities such as counting beads, building blocks, sorting objects, etc. will help to develop arithmetic abilities among mentally retarded children. Play way method is very useful and effective in training mentally retarded children.

Mentally retarded children should also be trained about money and its value, time concepts, problem solving and decision making abilities which are important to function as independent as possible.

Behaviour Modification Programme

Behaviour modification is a technique wherein environmental events are arranged so as to produce a specific change in observable behaviour (Ullmann and Krasner, 1965; O'heary and O'heary, 1977 and others). The general term behaviour modifications are often used to include more specific terms, such as operant conditioning, contingency management, contingency contracting, and behavioural modelling. Mentally retarded children often exhibit undesirable behaviour and sometimes they lack desirable behaviour. Behaviour modification programme should find an important place in the educational programme designed for them. Behaviour modification programme makes mentally retarded children to exhibit socially acceptable behaviour. Sometimes they are very aggressive and their behaviours are uncontrolled by any others. For such children behaviour modification programme is a vital one. Target behaviour is set and behaviour modification therapy is provided to modify that behaviour. Target behaviour is the behaviour we wish to modify, and it is important that we define behaviour quite specifically. To properly apply behavioural approaches, it is important to plan and specify contingencies in advance. Contingencies are relationships between behaviours and whatever events follow the behaviour. Contingency contracting is a process where such contingencies are part of a written contract. It has value at all age levels, but has been particularly useful at the upper-elementary and the secondary levels.

I. Reducing or Eliminating Undesirable Behaviour

Undesirable behaviour should be reduced or eliminated by- positive reinforcement of desirable behaviour, shaping, the use of contracts, token-reinforcement systems, modelling. All of them are effective depending upon the situation. However, there are four approaches to the reduction or elimination of undesirable behaviour. They are: the use of extinction, time out response cost, and punishment.

(a) *Extinction:* Extinction is a procedure for reducing behaviour that involves abruptly terminating the positive reinforcer (i.e.) maintaining an inappropriate target behaviour (Alberto and Troutman, 1982, p. 212). Extinction can be very effective for reducing school-related behaviours that are unacceptable. One of the greatest strengths is that it is more long lasting than all other approaches. It is very effective when used in combination with other procedures (positive reinforcement of desired behaviour modelling). Sulzer and Mayer (1972) note that to maximize the effectiveness of extinction we must I) identify all reinforcers for the response and withhold completely, 2) maintain the procedure long enough to show effect, and 3) provide reinforcement for other behaviours (p. 234). This procedure permits us to avoid the use of punishment.

(b) *Time Out:* It is a procedure used to reduce inappropriate behaviour. Time out is usually considered as a separate procedure for reducing inappropriate behaviour but may also be considered by some as a type of punishment (Alberto and Troutman 1982). It include placement outside the room in the hall or in an established 'time-out room'. It is a negative procedure so care should be taken while using it. To maximize its effectiveness, Sulzer and Mayer recommend the following: 1) remember to remove all reinforces, for all responses 2) apply consistently, 3) avoid time out from situations that are aversive, 4) use short time-out periods whenever possible and 5) provide reinforcement for any of several alternative behaviours.

Recommendations for use of Time-Out Procedures

1. The teacher should have identified the reinforcers that are maintaining the inappropriate behaviour.
2. Behaviours that will lead to time out should be explicitly stated in advance and clearly understood by the student.
3. All other forms of behaviour management should be exhausted before resorting to seclusion time out.
4. The teacher should develop a concise, written statement of procedures for use in placing a student in time-out. This statement might include the following:

    Explain behaviours that will result in time out in advance. Then when implementing, just say, "Mike, because you ____________ you are going to time-out for ____________ minutes".

    To assist students to assume responsibility for their actions, they should be given an opportunity to take their own time out.

    Time-out periods should be brief (i.e. one to five minutes) in nearly all cases,

When a seclusion time-out space is used, it should be

1. atleast six feet × six feet
2. Properly lighted and ventilated.
3. Free of fixtures, objects, etc. with which the student might possibly arm himself or herself.
4. continuously monitorable.
5. unlocked.

5. Complete records of time-out utilization should be maintained, including such data as time, date, length of time in time out, cause of time out, other procedures used.
6. A school advisory committee should be used to evaluate the use and effectiveness of time-out procedures and make recommendations as appropriate.

[Adapted from D. Gast and M. Nelson, "Time-out in the Classroom: Implications for Special Education". Exceptional children, 3 (1977), 461-64]

(c) *Response Cost:* Responses cost procedure are those in which reinforcers are removed as a consequence of inappropriate behaviours. Specific amounts of rewards must be removed for specified behaviour. This method is effective in reducing or eliminating undesirable behaviour. Students were given points or tokens at the start of each day, which may be exchanged for a variety of privileges or rewards. Then, if certain behaviours are exhibited students lose points. This system has proved effective in various research studies (Iwata and Bailey, 1974; Kazdin and Bootzin, 1972). In such systems, it is important that students should understand the rules.

(d) *Punishment:* Punishment has different meaning to different individual. Punishment is different from the time-out or response-cost procedures in that the

stimulus is presented, as opposed to something being withdrawn. Punishment should be avoided if possible, when used, punishment should be used effectively, not just to ease the tensions of the teacher. To be most effective, Sulzer and Mayer suggest that the following be observed: 1) prevent the student from escaping the situation, 2) apply punishment consistently, 3) maximize the intensity of the aversive stimulus, 4) combine with extinction, 5) combine with positive reinforcement of alternative behaviours, and 6) be certain the student understands the rules applied.

Thus, with the use of extinction, time-out, response-cost and punishment one can reduce or eliminate undesirable behaviour exhibited by the mentally retarded individual.

II. Increasing or Developing Desirable Behaviour

Desirable and acceptable behaviours are developed and increased by using various techniques or methods. Positive reinforcement is the most effective method in reducing undesirable behaviour and in increasing desirable behaviour. Positive reinforcement requires a contingent stimulus that will maintain or increase the targeted responses.

Reinforces are of three types. They are primary reinforcer, conditioned reinforcer and token reinforcer.

(a) *Primary reinforcers:* Include food, water, sex, warmth and similar life maintaining or perpetuating stimuli. Sulzer and Mayer (1972) points out that when a teacher waits for her class to line up quietly before they may go to the lunchroom, she is using food as a primary reinforcer for orderly behaviour.

(b) *Conditioned Reinforcers:* These are also effective in many cases. According to Sulzer and Mayer (1972), "A conditional reinforcer is a stimulus, an object or an event that initially was neutral but, through frequent pairings with primary or strong conditioned reinforcers, has assumed reinforcing properties". Axelrod (1977) notes that although there is a tendency to view conditioned reinforcers as something less than "real" reinforcers, they are quiet potent and are an important source of reinforcement in the school. Pairing of smiles, praise, pats and comments like 'good' excellent with primary reinforcers are a strong reinforcement in establishing or increasing desirable behaviour.

(i) *Token Reinforces:* Token reinforcers are simply a special kind of conditioned reinforcer, one that is particularly applicable in the classroom. Tokens might include stars, check marks, poker chips, trading stamps, or anything that the student recognizes as representing real value which are exchangeable for any of a variety of other items, activities or privileges. Whatever the token, the backup reinforcer is highly important. According to Lahey and Drabman (1981) certain reinforcers are of more value at specific ages. For example, mentally retarded children respond well to activities such as running errands, cleaning the room, or serving as a teaching assistant, candy, small toys, or trinkets ate also valuable.

(ii) *Modelling:* Modelling and positive reinforcement go hand in hand. Modelling is of value in modifying the frequency of previously learned responses or in the development of new responses (Rosenthal and Bandura, 1978). Modelling has implications in changing a students social behaviour.

(iii) *Shaping:* Shaping, like modelling is more often used with other types of behaviour modification. In shaping, we must carefully define the terminal behaviour we want and then plan the small steps which will likely lead to that behaviour. Also we have to provide appropriate reinforcement contingencies to reinforce the child. Negative reinforcement is one possible way to increase the frequency of whatever behaviour is the target of the behavioural procedure. Negative reinforcement is effective because the student performs the desired behaviour to avoid or escape the negative consequence.

(iv) *Prompting:* Physical guidance of mentally retarded individuals to perform a task or activity facilitate their independence. This action is reinforced. Prompting is effective in teaching self help skills. Acquisition of self help skills are very quick with the help of prompting.

(v) *Cueing:* When the trainers are using prompting cueing is combined. When he physically guides the children. In language training visual cues, and gestural cues with prompting are very useful.

(vi) *Fading:* Fading is nothing but when an individual learners to do something the trainer gradually fades out prompting and cueing.

The aforesaid techniques help the teacher to increase or develop desirable behaviour among mentally retarded children.

Record-Keeping

Once Individualized Educational Programme plan was drawn based on the abilities and current level of performance, the teacher carries out record keeping. This is useful in delineating the progress made by the child with the various use of instructional strategies. The evaluation of the instructional strategies and the development of the children's ability and performance are clearly known from the records. There are various forms of record keeping-recording the progress with equal interval of time and annual record writing. Records written with small interval of time helps to change the instructional methods in order to produce progress.

Annual record gives clear picture about the child's progress and attainment of set goals/objectives. Long-term goal is assessed by annual records. Short-term goals are assessed based on records of equal interval of time. Based on this record child's ability is known and this helps a teacher to set new objectives and develop new long term and short-term goals.

Summary

On the whole, teachers cannot develop a valuable educational programme without providing better placement service based on the child's ability and needs. There are many educational placement options such as—Regular classroom, Special class, Special day school, Home based instruction and Custodial care or Hospital care and Residential institutions. Recently, community based residential service delivery options are also in use. Once placement service is provided Individualised Educational Programme for mentally retarded children based on their needs can be organised. They may differ in their rate of skill acquisition, ability to attend to task, memory, generalisation and transfer of recently acquired skills and language development. So there arise a need to have different educational programme for each group. Each individual in a group also differ in their need's and ability. This necessitates the need for individualised educational programme for the group. Educable mentally retarded can learn basic academic skills and able to perform basic daily living skills independently. Trainable mentally retarded are in need of functional academic skills to be economically independent. The programme should also find a place for language, motor, social development, self-help skills training and yoga therapy. Health and safety skills, work habits and skills for diversional activities should also be a part and parcel of educational programme for trainable mentally retarded.

Various instructional methods/strategies such as tell-them method, model-it method, develop-it method, perceptual cueing strategies, language cueing strategies, reading strategies and written strategies can be used to deliver designed educational programme for the mentally retarded.

In behaviour modification programme, techniques like extinction, time out procedures, response cost, and punishment are used to reduce the undesirable behaviour. To increase desirable behaviour reinforcement token system, modelling, shaping, prompting and fading are some of the methods used by the teachers and practitioners.

Record keeping helps to know the child's progress and record the feedback of the instruction used by the teachers and practitioners. Records also help them to frame new objectives, long and short term goals for a child. These are some of the process involved in educating mentally retarded children.

5

Social Development in Mentally Retarded

OBJECTIVES

This chapter delineates the importance of social development, perspectives in social development and ways and means of developing social development. After reading this chapter the readers will be able to know:

1. The importance of social development;
2. Different perspectives in social development;
3. The ways and means of developing social competency in children with mental retardation and various intervention strategies.

Introduction

Social development helps to function effectively in a social environment and strengthens interpersonal relationships which are mutually beneficial to the individuals well being and that of others. Variety of social agents, or determinants helps for an effective social interaction. Social development helps in sex-role identity and social standards and a sense of conscience. Incorporation of external social agents through social integration by the students helps to construct programmes that facilitate appropriate behaviour in other social situations. Children's are active participants in the environment rather than passive recipients in their acquisition of social behaviours.

Social and cultural system of the children influences social development. Based on the cultural backgrounds and on parental beliefs related to the nature of children how they should behave, as adults the children are enculturated differently. Children's acquisition of social trails and skills is independent of culture and that the process of social development is similar across cultures and social systems (Garwood 1983).

Socialization is aimed to acquire pro-social behaviours that help to bring people together and diminish social distance. Periodical behaviours are actions that aid or benefit another person or group of persons without the anticipation of external reward (Mussen and Eisenberg-Berg, 1977). Pro-social behaviours are altruism, nurturance, co-operation, and participation in activities that reduce social injustices, inequities and brutality, whereas, antisocial behaviour disrupts interpersonal behaviours. Behaviours like aggression, anger, and hostility and acting out behaviours leads to antisocial behaviours. This inturn increases social distance.

As a mentally retarded child there arise a need to develop better social interactions. This inturn facilitates to have better interpersonal relationships. Social competence is one of the important skills that have to be developed among retarded individual for better rehabilitation.

Social Development

Social development occurs in children in different social contexts. Sociologists, and social scientists, explain this social development in children from different perspectives. A close look at such perspectives will give better idea about social development in children. There are so many theoretical approaches to enhance social interactions. They are discussed here under. Theoretical perspectives to explain social development are evolved from two viewpoints—learning theory and developmental theory. According to the learning theoretics view children's social behaviours are shaped by environmental experiences whereas, the developmentalists view social development as a continuous and active process of change and refinement in which children's behaviours increasingly more complex, mature and refined.

Learning Theory Perspective-Social Learning Theory

Learning-theory approach to social development is the influence of external factors (positive and negative reinforcement) on social behaviours. Parents and teachers shape their children's social behaviours.

The traditional learning-theory approach to social development relies on external environmental factors, i.e. stimulation and reinforcement, which are the determinants of behaviour. The student is a passive recipient of these external factors. Antecedent and consequent events helps in social development as they are related to a particular response.

Traditional learning-theorists conceptualize social development as a learning process in which new social skills and abilities are acquired primarily because performance of these behaviours is rewarded by a person in the child's environment. Those behaviours that are not valued by a particular social system may be punished or at least go unrewarded—consequently, non valued behaviours slowly drop out of a child's behavioural repertoire.

Social Learning Theory is a relatively new theoretical framework, which is an outgrowth of the learning-theory perspective (Garwood, 1983). Observational learning in social situations for acquiring new behaviours is focused in social learning theory. Modelling and imitation plays important role in social development. Accordingly learning is a combination of psychological principles and social conditions, learning that occurs through observation results from manipulation of internal cognitive variables (Miller, 1983). Social learning theorists' believe that they can observe some one's behaviour and acquire new knowledge without actual performance. According to them reinforcement is not needed for learning, but rather, observation teaches the possible consequences of behaviour. Learning is a cognitive process that is influenced by observation and modelling. Children learn from both live models and symbolic models. They acquire information in the form of symbolic representation of modelled activities. Verbal mediation or instruction is also a form of symbolic modelling, which is translated into overt behaviour.

Observation and imitation of other's social behaviours helps to acquire social skills. The reciprocal interaction of children with the environment results in behaviour change. Social learning theory integrates operant conditioning and reinforcement with socialization and information processing. Basis for abstract behavioural norms are students accurate learning by cognitive capacities (attention and retention) and reinforcement. Performance of social skills is determined by the accuracy of students' learning.

The quality of social development results from the appropriate social behaviour emitted by others in a child's environment. Children imitate their parents in the early socialization process. Parents are the most consistent and salient models of behaviour and dispensers of reinforcement. If children are exposed to undesirable modes of behaviour and excessive forms of punishment they will have difficulty in adapting to societal norms. Socialization during early childhood is critically important to children's overall development.

Children's early prosocial behaviour can be strengthened with the use of reinforcement. If children are rewarded by praise, attention, or gifts for sharing or helping others in distress, these early responses will be strengthened and the likelihood of their subsequent repetition is increased. As children become older, most prosocial urges, such as helping and generosity, appear to be controlled internally without any apparent external rewards. It may be assumed that the original controls were extrinsic, however, behaviour soon becomes independent of external sanctions, and children administer their own rewards and punishment consequently, children learn the responses, which bring external praise and they begin to reinforce actions. They gradually acquire an internal cognitive representation of external rewards and are able to exercise control over their own behaviours; that is praise themselves for those they construct values and guidelines needed for self-regulation.

Developmental Theory Viewpoint

Social development from developmental viewpoint will include the psychodynamic theories of Freud (1924) and

Erikson, (1968) and the social-cognitive theories of Piaget (1932) and Kohlberg (1963). Developmental theory attempts to explain the course of development through a set of general principles or rules that specify the antecedents for change and identify those variables that modify the rate or nature of change (Miller 1983).

(a) Psychodynamic Theory (1924)

The psychodynamic theory of Sigmund Freud conceptualised human development in terms of unconscious motivation, which provides the impetus for behaviour. From this perspective, social development is the acquisition of skills and abilities to control these unconscious motivational forces in a socially acceptable manner. According to Freud children's early lives have great influence on their development. He was especially concerned with parents reactions to children's emotions of fear, anger, love and sexuality. Freud also believed that there was a natured sequence of events to govern the expression of emotions and the acquisition of controls over these emotions. Freud's theoretical perspective was rich with ideas concerning children's social development. He focused on children's internalization of parental or adult standards of behaviour through identification—a defence mechanism in which children resolve conflicts by inculcating the adult standards of those they emulate—and on the superego, or conscience, which enables children, by themselves, to perform some of their parental or adult-controlled functions. Identification influences the internalization and incorporation of humanistic values and patterns of pro-social behaviours, as do parental and societal prohibitions (Mussen and Eisenberg-Berg 1977). Their children adopt parent's nurturant, generous and altruistic characteristics.

(b) Psycho-social Theory: Erik Erikson (1968)

Erik Erikson is an ego psychologist, who deemphasized Freud's biological approach and focused on the impact of societal influence on social development (Miller 1983). Erikson's theory presents a comprehensive social matrix that consists of the child, mother and father, other primary caretakers, the extended family, and the child's historical and cultural heritage. Erikson believes that to become a fully functioning social individual, it is important to develop the ego capabilities inherent in a particular stage during developmental stage. If childhood crises are not handled satisfactorily, the person continues to struggle in later life.

Erikson's theory highlights the effects of social influences and environmental forces that interface as children evolve into total functioning and unique personalities. The following table outlines some inappropriate behavioural manifestations of students who have not acquired the necessary ego capabilities at Erikson's first five stages of psycho-social development and suggestions for teachers when working with these students.

Characteristic Behaviours and Suggested Environmental Adoption

Erikson's Stage	Intervention Strategies
Trust Vs Mistrust	
Unable to discriminate appropriate behaviours in a social setting	Teach appropriate social strategies and help students "walk through" behaviour.
Gullible and unsure of self.	Develop a sense of self-trust by providing successful experiences.
Continually "testing" others, responsiveness.	Self limits within safe boundaries and allow choices for decision making.
Autonomy Vs. Shame and Doubt	
Inability to complete tasks and destruction of products	Structured environment of natural consequences with clear behavioural expectations required finished products.
Defies authority and disruptive outbursts.	Define boundaries and means of expressing self within boundaries.
Intolerance of frustration inability to control self or to tolerate control of others.	Design work within students' capabilities provides success which leads to self-esteem and pride.
	Establish one-to-one working relationship and simple peer activities and role-playing to allow for expression of opinions.

Initiative Vs Guilt

Energy is stiffed guilt over goals leads to lack of lest and disinterest in exploration dependent and unable to assume responsibility for behaviour.	Reinforce exploration develop realistic goals that lead to success and provide opportunities for practice in an enriched and varied environment.
	Decision making activities within a structured environment.

Industry Vs Inferiority

Low esteem and apathetic—sense of worthlessness and isolation.	Create successful climate in which industry is an acceptable goal.
Rebellious and aggressive attempts to create self-worth.	Avoid comparative grading; positive feedback for initiative and co-operation.
Over dependence on others and need for approval.	Avoid reinforcing rebellious behaviours teach strategies for self-control and self-worth. Accept efforts within judgement, teach strategies to attain learning goals independently.

Identity Vs Role Confusion

Peer group dominates, tendency to over identity, little sense of self; total conformity.	Develop positive peer culture and awareness and understanding of behaviours.
Delinquent behaviour and switching group allegiance.	Discussions about various role models, present positive and negative alternatives.
Erratic mood swings and feelings of aggression or depression.	Supportive and knowledgeable teacher, who is human and trustworthy and supports emotional changes.
People viewed as "good" or "bad"- no grey areas.	Discussions about moral issues and dilemmas to increase awareness of differences of different perspectives.
	Student-initiated/centered activities that foster personal exploration evaluation.

(c) Jean Piaget's Moral Development (1932)

According to Piaget there were two stages in moral development—moral heteronomy and moral autonomy—which are linked by a transition period. Moral heteronomy characterizes children whose thinking is below the level of concrete operations. Rules that are fixed and absolute is maintained by the younger children and obey it by some prestigious authority. Rules an external to the child's mind and followed by them unconditionally. Children's moral development and moral judgements is based on the adult authority or the law commands and the consequences (reinforcement and punishments) of behaviour but not on intentions or motivations for behaviour. Moral reasoning is characterized by the absoluteness of their values and their belief that everything is either totally right or wrong and that punishment for behavioural transgressions will be severe.

Young children's moral reasoning is understood by their cognitive structures. Young children are very ego centric, their thoughts are realistic; they conceive psychological phenomena such as thoughts, dreams and rules as physical entities.

Moral autonomy occurs during the pre adolescent years as students enter the formal operational stage of cognitive development. This stage is characterized by moral relativism or morality of co-operation in which equity dominates student's thinking about justice. Adolescents reject arbitrary punishments, moral absolutism, and blind obedience to authority. Maturation and autonomous concepts of justice results from decentration during adolescent stage. This permits them to recognize another's perspective, and results in co-operation and reciprocity among peers. As our concern for others, welfare and rights increases it diminishes ego-centrism. Authority figures does not excise among peers, and they develop ideas of equality, co-operation, and solidarity. According to Piaget, moral thinking of a child gets matured as they mature. However, children do not seem to progress through orderly sequences of moral development as they do with cognitive development.

(d) Lawrence Kohlberg's Moral Development (1969)

Piaget's initial formulations are amplified in the Kohlberg's theory of moral development. According to Kohlberg's, person's level of cognitive development such as thinking and reasoning is important in moral maturity. Child's moral reasoning is based on the cognitive judgemental processes of classification, grouping, and conservation. Educational implications from Piagetian and Kohlbergian emphasize increasing students' moral reasoning abilities to a level of moral autonomy. Exchange alternative points of view and to consider others' perspectives as prerequisites for constructing moral values needed for decision making and pro-social behaviour should be encouraged among students. Moral autonomy should be developed among students. For that, students should acquire mutual affection and respect for one another and the significant adults in their environments. This may be developed by creating a climate of positive social interaction in which students exchange viewpoints, interpret and evaluate others' ideas and develop relationships among their own thoughts and values. They respect the rules and goals they make for themselves, and they work hard to attain those goals (Kamii 1984).

Developing Social Competence among Mentally Retarded

Very often mentally retarded students behave inappropriately in social situations and are rejected and isolated by their peers. They are socially incompetent and unable to deal with life's challenges and respond effectively to the society.

The concept of competence implies that socially skilled persons can recognize that social situations require the differential use of social patterns and sequences, determine the appropriateness of specific social skills, and perform in a socially acceptable manner that increases the likelihood that the behaviour will result in positive consequences (Deshler and Schumaker 1983). The socially competent person are those motivated to have social goals, can perceive social situations by attending to social cues and stimuli, can interpret and assign meaning to social patterns and sequences, and can perform the appropriate behaviours within the specific social context. In addition, they are sensitive to social feedback and can integrate that feedback to enhance further, acceptable social interaction (Kronick 1983; Deshler and Schumaker, 1983).

An emphasis on the improvement of students' social skills and competencies should assist them to profit from their educational experiences, to function more efficiently in mainstreamed settings, and to increase their employability (Deshler and Schumaker 1983).

Mentally retarded student's inappropriate social behaviour may result from incorrect perceptions of social situations. Incorrect perceptions may be due to the difficulties they have in selective attention and inhibition. They have also problems in detecting and understanding contextual clues, situations. They are also unable to identify emotional and social relationships and to understand other's thoughts, feelings, and perceptions. They may lack imagery of sequence and an understanding of cause-effect relationships in social situations. Quite often such students have not learned the appropriate behaviour for specific situations and the need for differential conversation with adults and peers. They may not notice how people respond to their behaviour and may misconstrue social detail and inflection (Kronick 1983; Pearl, Bryan and Donahue 1983). Mentally retarded individuals who have deficit in syntactic structures and in generating and retrieving vocabulary to express themselves may also affect their ability to communicate. These language deficits also cause awkward social interactions and make an individual less skilful in maintaining conversations.

A typical conversation practices are often responsible for the students' lack of popularity and rejection by their peers (Pearl, Bryan, and Donahue 1983). They may also possess the appropriate skills and strategies, but they do not know which behaviour is appropriate for the situation. They can also verbalize the attitude concerning pro-social behaviour but they do not know how to use them. In this case, they need a structured learning situation and direct instruction concerning behaviours relevant to specific settings.

Intervention Strategies for Developing Social Competence

Intervention strategies play an important role in developing appropriate behaviour and positive mental health. Various instructional methodologies and management techniques are designed for mentally retarded individual to develop socially acceptable behaviours. These students may require specific instruction in social situations to facilitate the organization of incoming stimuli and outgoing responses. Intervention must be planned based on full knowledge of student's total environment. Quite often mentally retarded individuals' inappropriate behaviour in social situations yields negative responses and attention from their peers. They seem to be lacking in self-control, ego strength, and social personal adjustment, which is necessary for establishing positive interpersonal relationships. Therefore, there is a need to design educational interventions that emphasize social and interpersonal skill development to help students to acquire pro-social behaviours.

(i) Psycho-educational Intervention

Students' cognitive performance is enhanced by mastery of affective experiences, which inturn are influenced by intellectual mastery (Fagen and Long 1979; Fagen, Long and Stevens 1975). Quite often, mentally retarded individuals are not able to identify their affective states or feelings because they are unable to generate and to retrieve appropriate words to express those feelings. Psycho-educational intervention is holistic and relies on student's attitudes, interests and skills, and their active involvement in learning. Psycho-educational intervention helps to integrate thoughts and feelings and stimulate the constructive expression of affective experiences needed for appropriate social interaction and academic achievement.

Psycho-educational perspective is the foundation for crisis intervention and life-space interview techniques (Morse 1971, Redl 1959), reality therapy (Glasser, 1975), the self-control curriculum (Fagen, Long and Stevens 1975) and social learning/ therapy (Goldstein 1981), Goldstein et al. 1980, 1979) each of which helps students to develop positive feelings and internal control over their behaviour.

(ii) Crisis Intervention

Crisis intervention focuses on managing students surface behaviours while simultaneously dealing with the deeper meaning of the incident. Students have to cope up with stressful situation for their growth and change. This can be carried out by verbal intervention and environmental manipulation, this inturn help them to cope with academic and social pressures. Intervention may be of life-space interview or remedial instruction. Morse (1971) believes that the person who conducts the life-space interview must be well versed in interviewing techniques and the skills necessary to effect behavioural change.

(iii) Life-Space Interview

Redl (1959) and Morse (1976) developed a technique life-space interview, which helps an adult to make students to understand the effects of their unconscious thoughts and feelings and the actions of others. This technique centres on a crisis when and where it occurs and is intended to help students gain insight into a problem and develop positive alternatives for dealing with situation that culminate in conflict and crisis. It helps the students to understand and to cope up with stress.

Life space interview consists of as many as seven steps (Morse, 1976), which help the students, understand and cope up the conflict.

1. Investigating conditions
2. Testing depth and spread
3. Content clarification
4. Acceptance of feelings
5. Avoiding Value Judgements
6. Exploration of internal mechanisms
7. Two resolution phase.

The aforesaid steps may be modified according to the students need. A related technique includes reality therapy as a means of managing disruptive classroom behaviours.

(iv) Reality Therapy

It is a specialized learning process that helps students to face reality and fulfil responsibility for meeting the two basic needs: Love and self-esteem. It focuses on changing students overt behaviour which is realistic responsible and right.

Long term impact and consequences of personal actions are recognized in realistic behaviour. The life-long acquisition of responsibility is a complicated process in which we learn to behave according to acceptable societal standards. The right wrong aspects of reality therapy refer to people's inappropriate rationalisations, justifications, and other exploitative activities that mature their inappropriate behaviour.

(v) Self Control Curriculum

Self control curriculum is a process oriented approach that develops affective skills which inturn facilitates skills to cope flexibly and realistically with life's situations. It also teaches them to have better feelings about themselves and to appreciate others feelings. Fagen, Long and Stevens (1975) believe that students capacity for self control depends on cognitive-and affective-skill clusters that enable them to direct and regulate personal actions in a flexible and realistic manner. Self control curriculum facilitate the acceptance and expression of feelings as alternatives to destructive behaviour, develops new positive learning, creating awareness and increasing constructive feelings in contrast with negative and unproductive ones and promote mutual understanding and problem solving. Role playing, games and discussions are some of the strategies to direct and regulate their behaviour flexibly and realistically.

Games: Games have lasting impressions, greater learning potential and changes to suit the group's wishes. Games develop imaginative and exciting learning activities.

Role Playing: Role playing method promotes flexibility and imagination in role identification and facilitates realistic and effective learning experience. It makes students to manage and appreciate personal feelings and frustration, to anticipate consequences and accept other's viewpoint. It also promotes decision making which is related to self esteem and perceived control over situations. Discussion is the presentation of academic content and other information in small groups or on an individual basis.

Fagen, Long and Stevens (1975) suggested self control curriculum for implementing a Psycho-educational approach to instruction for the development of students' cognitive and affective needs. They provide specific goals, objectives and learning activities to facilitate cognitive processes (attention, perception, memory cognition and expression) and affective experiences (appreciating feelings, managing frustrations and inhibitions and learning to relax). The following table provides an overview of the self-control curriculum and instructional units:

The Self Control Curriculum: Overview of Curriculum Areas and Units

Curriculum Area/Defined	Instructional Units
Selection: accurate perception	1. Focussing and concentration
	2. Mastering figure ground discrimination
	3. Mastering distractions and interferences
Storage: retention of information	1. Developing visual memory
	2. Developing auditory memory
Sequencing and ordering: organising and planning actions	1. Developing time orientation
	2. Developing auditory-visual sequencing
	3. Developing sequential planning
Anticipating consequences: relating actions to outcomes	1. Developing alternatives
	2. Evaluating consequences
Appreciating feelings: Identification and constructive use of affective experiences	1. Identifying feelings
	2. Developing positive feelings
	3. Managing feelings
	4. Reinterpreting feeling events
Managing frustration: coping with negative feelings	1. Accepting feelings of frustration
	2. Building coping resources
	3. Tolerating frustration

Inhibition and delay: postponing actions	1. Controlling action 2. Developing partial goals
Relaxation: reducing internal tensions	1. Developing body relaxation 2. Developing thought relaxation 3. Developing movement relaxation

(vi) Social Learning Therapy

Social competence must be learned through social interaction. It is not developed through formal teaching. Even then, teacher is also responsible for the continued development of social skills and effective application of academic skills. It should be a continuation of topics dealt with at the junior high school level, but it should be in terms of the present developmental levels and needs of the youth participating in the programme. Social experiences, social drama and role playing and discussions to develop understanding of the kinds of behaviour that are desirable and acceptable in various social situations are provided for the development of social skills. Respect for authority, consideration of others, good manners and a degree of responsibility should find place in the training programme for the mentally retarded to promote better social development.

To attain the goal of mainstreaming social competence plays a vital role. The curriculum for mentally retarded children must emphasize socialisation as an important skill that should be developed.

Goldstein (1981), Goldstein, Spraftkin, Gershaw, and Klein (1980) and Goldstein, Sprafkin and Gershaw (1979) believe that students need help in dealing with feelings of stress and aggression and in developing social planning skills to facilitate their interaction with peers, parents and teachers. They have designed a psycho-educational intervention called structured learning therapy, which focuses on developing students' pro-social interpersonal and stress management/ coping skills and also confidence in their abilities to resolve conflict. Modelling, role playing, performance feedback, and transfer of training are the components of social skill training.

They listed out the forty nine skills in social learning therapy of social skills curriculum. The listed skills are grouped under six headings such as: Beginning social skills, Advanced social skills, Skills for dealing with feelings, Skill alternatives, Skills for dealing with stress, and Planning skills. The sub skills under each group are mentioned here under.

Social Skill Curriculum

Group 1: Beginning Social Skills

1. Listening
2. Starting a conversation
3. Having a conversation
4. Asking a question
5. Saying thank you
6. Introducing yourself
7. Introducing other people
8. Giving a compliment

Group II: Advanced Social Skills

9. Asking for help
10. Joining in
11. Giving instructions
12. Following instructions
13. Apologizing
14. Convening others

Group III: Skills for Dealing with Feelings

15. Knowing your feelings
16. Expressing your feelings
17. Understanding the feelings of others
18. Dealing with someone else's anger
19. Expressing affection
20. Dealing with fear
21. Rewarding yourself

Group IV: Skill Alternatives

22. Asking permission
23. Sharing something
24. Helping others
25. Negotiation
26. Using self-control
27. Standing up for your rights
28. Responding to teasing
29. Avoiding trouble with others
30. Keeping out of fights

Group V: Skills for dealing with Stress

31. Making a complaint
32. Answering a complaint
33. Sportsmanship after the game
34. Dealing with embarrassment
35. Dealing with being left out
36. Standing up for a friend
37. Responding to persuasion
38. Responding to failure
39. Dealing with contradictory messages
40. Dealing with an accusation
41. Getting ready for a difficult conversation
42. Dealing with group pressure

Group VI: Planning Skills

43. Deciding on something to do
44. Deciding what caused a problem
45. Setting a goal
46. Deciding on your abilities
47. Gathering information

48. Arranging problems by importance
49. Concentrating on task

    (Adapted from A.P. Goldstein, R.P. Sprafkin N.J. Gershaw and P. Klein. Skill streaming the Adolescent. 'A Structured Learning Approach to Teaching Prosocial Skills. Campaign, III: Research Press, co., 1980.)

Summary

Social development strengthens interpersonal relationships, which allows an individual to function effectively within a social environment. Effective social interaction takes place by a variety of social agents, or determinants. Students actively incorporate the standards of external social agents through their social interaction. Social development is influenced by social and cultural system. Even then, social development is also strengthened by various learning theory perspective views that children's social behaviours are shaped by parents and teachers. This approach relies on external environmental factors. Social learning theory is a new theoretical framework, which is an outgrowth of the learning theory perspective. According to this theory modelling and imitation plays important role in social development. Observation, and imitation of other's social behaviours helps to acquire social skills. Children's pro-social behaviour can be strengthened with the use of reinforcement. Developmentalists viewpoint include the psycho-dynamic theories of Freud and Erikson and the social cognitive theories of Piaget and Kohlberg. Piagets moral development namely-Moral heteronomy and moral autonomy explains social development. Kohlberg's moral judgement is amplified by Piaget's moral development. According to him social development or moral maturity is developed by a person's level of cognitive development such as thinking and reasoning. Mentally retarded are socially incompetent and unable to deal with life's challenges and respond effectively to them. Emphasis on the improvement of students' social skills and competencies should assist them to profit from their educational experiences to function more efficiently in mainstreamed settings and to increase their employability. Mentally retarded students inappropriate social behaviour may result from incorrect perceptions of social situations. Language deficits also cause awkward social interactions and make an individual less skilful in maintaining conversations.

Various instructional methodologies and management techniques are designed for mentally retarded individual to develop socially acceptable behaviours. Intervention must be planned based on full knowledge of students' total environment. Psycho-educational intervention helps to integrate thoughts and feelings and stimulate the constructive expression of affective experiences needed for appropriate social interaction and academic achievement. Crisis intervention, life-space interview, reality therapy, self-control curriculum and social learning therapy helps in social development. Teacher plays a vital role in the development of social skills. The curriculum for social development should be in terms of present developmental levels and needs of the child. This training in turn facilitate to attain effective mainstreaming.

6

Career Education, Vocational Rehabilitation and Counselling Services

OBJECTIVES

This chapter aimed at career education and counselling activities for dealing with mentally retardation. After reading this chapter the readers will be able to:

1. Know the various career education models;
2. Know the vocational rehabilitation programmes for the mentally retarded;
3. Understand the concept of counselling, the ways and means of providing counselling to parents, peer group and community.

Introduction

Career education makes education more relevant to the economic and employment realities of the day. Career educational curriculum meets the life needs, and help students to be economically independent. Career education is the combination of both academic and occupational orientation to education. This career education is a developmental process that begins in childhood and continues throughout one's life. Career education has been defined as 'the totality of experiences through which one learns about and prepares to engage in work as part of one's way of living' (Hoyt, 1975). Career education involves three distinct phases or stages. They are—career awareness, career exploration and career preparation. Career awareness stage is nothing but developing the values of working and the different types of work during the elementary years. Career exploration shifts its focus on learning about specific occupations and the relationship of various occupational roles to the personal interest, aptitudes and abilities of the individual. Career preparation, stage starts in higher secondary. It stresses the selection of specific occupational and vocational roles, which relates to the personal interest, aptitude ability and also with the life style that the individual desires. Brolin (1982) has proposed a fourth stage of career education: the career placement/follow up/continuing education stage. Career education has been enthusiastically endorsed by special educators. A major purpose of special education is to prepare handicapped individuals to lead productive, personally satisfying adult lives, to become a self-sustaining and as a contributing member of society. Making mentally retarded individual to succeed at home, in school and in community does not depend on academic training but also on training for good work habits, appropriate socio-personal behaviour and in independent living skills.

Career education helps mentally retarded to achieve normalization. Normalization is the concept that all handicapped persons should be provided with the opportunity to live according to the patterns and conditions of every day life, which are as close as possible to the norms and patterns of the mainstream society.

Career Education Models in Special Education

Earlier work study programmes was designed to serve primarily educable mentally retarded students. Although career education is a recent movement its roots run deep. It is also been specifically endorsed for students with sensory impairments as well as for the moderately and severely mentally retarded. There are three models of career education relevant to exceptional children. Among those models Brolin and

Kokaska's (1979) life-centered model and Clark's (1979) school-based model—were specifically designed to address the unique needs of handicapped learners. The third model, the experience based career education model, was developed for non-handicapped learners but is highly relevant to many exceptional learners.

(i) Clark's School Based Model

Kindergarten—through adulthood developmental nature of career education is depicted by Clark's school based career education model. There are four interrelated domains, which are a fundamental to career education. They are: 1) values, attitudes and habits 2) human relationships 3) occupational information and 4) acquisition of actual jobs and daily living skills. These domains should remain as an important feature of career education for exceptional students through the secondary school level. Clark maintains that the four domains should be stressed at the elementary level, which is a foundation for decision making and individual career achievement. This model address unique special education needs. It stresses the processes involved in developing personal values, attitudes, habits and human relationships. Clark (1979) suggested the following school based career education model for the handicapped.

(ii) Life-centered Competency-based Model

Brolin's (1978) life centered approach to career education has identified 22 competencies and 102 sub competencies in three curriculum areas: 1) daily living skills 2) personal-social skills and 3) occupational guidance and preparation skills. This approach stresses that the mildly handicapped student should have all these skills before leaving school. Because these competency statements encompass the skills everyone needs to succeed in community living. Competencies listed by Brolin's are given here under in three curriculum areas.

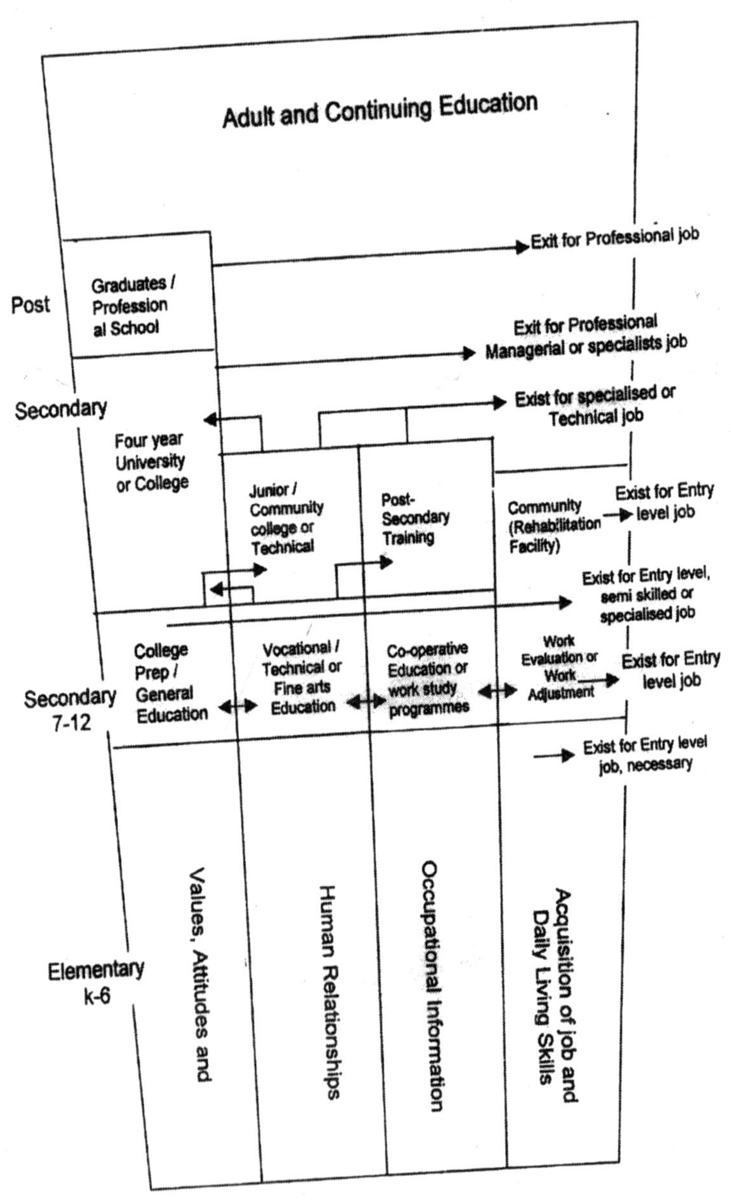

Clark's School Based Career Education Model (1979)

CAREER EDUCATION COMPETENCIES

A. Daily Living Skills Curriculum Area

1. Managing family finance
2. Caring for and repairing home furnishing and equipment
3. Caring for personal needs
4. Raising children, family living
5. Buying and preparing food
6. Buying and making clothing
7. Engaging in civic activities
8. Utilizing recreation and leisure
9. Mobility in the community

B. Personal Social Skills Curriculum Area

10. Achieving self awareness
11. Acquiring self-confidence
12. Achieving socially responsible behaviour
13. Maintaining good interpersonal relationships
14. Achieving independence
15. Making good decisions, problem solving
16. Communicating adequately with others

C. Occupational Guidance and Preparation Curriculum Area

17. Knowing and exploring occupational possibilities
18. Making appropriate occupational decisions
19. Exhibiting appropriate work behaviour
20. Exhibiting sufficient physical and manual skills.
21. Acquiring a specific suitable job. Skill is not included because the sub competencies would be unique to the particular skill being acquired.

22. Seeking, securing, and maintaining satisfactory employment.

The daily living skills curriculum area includes the skills needed to care for oneself, to participate in family living and to manage home and family finances. 'Care for personal needs', means to dress appropriately, what clothes to wear according to weather conditions, caring for clothes could be taught.

Personal-social skills curriculum area aims to foster self-understanding and independence. At the initial stage, students are made aware of important signs, such as traffic, safety and restroom signs. At the next stage, they are provided with the types of information in the newspaper and locating business and agencies by the usage of various modes such as multimedia, T.V. Radio, etc. In the career preparation stage students are made to explore and use help-wanted ads, newspaper advertisements and information directory pages to plan for real or simulated occupational or recreational pursuits.

Occupational guidance and preparation skills include various competencies that should be developed at various stages. Knowledge about job classification can be taught at all levels. In career awareness level emphasis can be on the variety of jobs that are available in the school or community. Identification and discussion on job classifications are trained at career exploration stage. Classification based on: by salary, type of work, level of skill, training required, and location of work is made known to students. At the career preparation stage students are made to participate in actual job training. Competency based model explains all the stages of career education and the integral involvement of the school, home and community.

(iii) Experience-based Career Education Model (EBCE)

This model is successful with non-handicapped, mildly handicapped, and gifted youngsters at secondary level. This model is highly structured, individualized and community based education, which attempts to relate it to the world of work. This programme involves community placements of 1 to 3 hours a day for 2 to 3 weeks each in work settings like bank, hospitals, travel agencies, factories, and in other job situations. Learning co-ordinator is responsible for selection of occupational placements and in providing related academic learning experiences. This is carried out in individualized approach. In community placements, students are given opportunities for observation and job related experiences. Larson (1982) has listed out five basic parameters of EBCE:

1. The programme must be community based;
2. Scheduling is highly individualized;
3. Employer participation is voluntary;
4. The experiences are exploratory in natural, not oriented toward specific occupational skill development;
5. Academics are developed in conjunction with the learning site.

As this model is highly structured of individualised, this is more appropriate career education model for mentally retarded children. High level of community involvement is needed in career education. So there is a need to integrate school, family and community.

Instructional Approaches in Career Education

Infusion and separate programming are the two approaches in career education instruction. Infusion approach integrates career education and the existing curriculum. Separate programming approach involve: 1) Separate curriculum for career education 2) Developing and conducting separate career education classes, or providing specific units to career education within courses on other subjects. This approach is the one used most frequently.

Infusion approach relates curriculum content to adult careers. This increases the relevance of education for the learner. Another method of infusing career education is stressing the relevance of regular subjects to the problems of earning a living and other aspects of life after graduation. In this method the focus of instruction is the academic subject matter. This type of method, instruction should implement:

Mathematics: Demonstrate practical applications of mathematical processes as in measuring money management, construction plans, and computing wages and deduction. Use a token economy to demonstrate the relationship between work tasks and earnings.

Language Arts: Children are made known how people use language in different occupations. Role playing method is useful in providing instruction to the students. Students are also made to write business and thank-you letters and use telephone. Various communication modes helps them to develop language abilities which is a must in work situation. Language codes interpersonal relationship between human beings in the immediate environment. So to be successfully rehabilitated in the work situation one has to possess good language abilities.

Social Studies: History and future of a job, business or industry should be made known. This helps them to examine the variety of jobs and services available in a community. Training in map reading is given to aid mobility which is very useful for the jobs like delivering and driving.

Health, Physical Education and Fine Arts: Need for oral hygiene, cleanliness and appropriate dressing and grooming is stressed. The appreciation of the arts and of aesthetics can be taught as a leisure time activity.

Clark (1979) suggests that students are served best through the use of a combination of the infusion and separate programming approaches. The combination approach permits a balance between academic skills and career education skills providing a unique opportunity to tie together the two sets of competencies (Clark, 1979). Preparation and orientation of the teachers involved and the schools commitment to career education determines the ratio of separate programming to infusion in any school programme.

Vocational Rehabilitation

Career Education is a much broader concept that encompasses vocational education, work attitudes and skills at secondary and post-secondary levels. Vocational education is centred on providing specific vocational skill training and vocational adjustment; whereas career education is concerned with the quality of the individuals total life adjustment.

The aim of special education is to prepare handicapped individual to lead productive, personally satisfying adult lives. Career education and vocational rehabilitation services for the mildly, moderately handicapped helps to achieve the said goal. Career education programme extend hand in these efforts. In an effort to increase the efficiency and effectiveness of vocational education for special needs students various types of vocational rehabilitation placement such as Open Employment and Sheltered Workshops are followed.

(i) Open Employment

In this type, the mentally retarded children are trained to work in various work situations within the community. To excel in this situation, they have to be trained to adjust with co-workers, exhibit good interpersonal relationships, better communication abilities, exhibit good manners in the work place etc. Mild mentally retarded children will function effectively in open workshop situations. They can be trained to co-operate well with co-workers, heads etc. For the person who can't function effectively in open workshop they can do well in the sheltered workshop.

(ii) Sheltered Workshops

In work place, even moderately and severely mentally retarded students are made vocationally rehabilitated to some extent. Here, they are trained to work under assistance or supervision. There may be supervisors and attenders to provide help to the students to do the work. Moderately and severely retarded students are trained to do repetitive jobs like cover making, pasting, sorting, packing etc.,

The students who may not able to work in the open employment/workshops will be effectively accommodated to work in the sheltered workshops. They will be paid according to their performance and efficiency level. Least restrictive environment is provided in this work situation, which helps mentally retarded individuals to work effectively.

Thus educational programme that combine training in academic, personal, social, daily living, and occupational skills makes the individual to excel. Once the mentally retarded individuals are able to work in sheltered workshop this will automatically facilitate them to work better in the open society in future.

Counselling Services

There are various counselling services available for mentally retarded. They are parent counselling, peer counselling and community counselling.

(I) Parent Counselling

Every parents aspire to have a healthy and a normal child. But when they have a disabled child all their expectations are vanished away. They try to make their child normal at any cost. For that they will take their child to all doctors. This process is known as doctors shopping. When this doesn't work out they believe in God and pray to make their child normal. They also pray that in return they pay their wealth.

It will take long period for any parent for accepting their child's disability. They exhibit various defence mechanism like denial, bargaining, rejecting, depression, and finally acceptance. They accept their child's disability because of their child's life long adjustment. In order to assist the parents in dealing effectively with this situation, counselling is essential, as a part of the whole management plan.

Counselling is the integral part of the services for the mentally retarded children/youth. The type of counselling given differ from other counselling situations, sin it does not cease at any stage, but continuous for the life span of the handicapped or till the parent feels that he can completely takeover the management and training of the child.

The main aims and objectives of counselling are:

1. To increase the awareness of the parent, that the child is handicapped children;

2. To help them to bear the shock and frustration associated with the knowledge that their child is handicapped and to accept their child;
3. To provide constructive methods of training and management of their handicapped children;
4. To give information regarding the existing services available for the handicapped children;
5. To give timely assistance during crisis periods;
6. To give anticipatory guidance;
7. To provide genetic counselling.
8. To provide information and guidance to the other members of the family in adjusting to the child, and managing him.

Duration of the Counselling Process

The duration of the counselling process and the frequency of the interview depend on several factors, which are:

1. The awareness and understanding of the parent;
2. The type of counselling and guidance involved;
3. The availability of other supportive services for the exceptional children.

In general, counselling of parents is a life-long process.

When Counselling should be given

Counselling and guidance should be available:

1. As early as the handicap can be detected, soon after the child has been assessed and diagnosis is made;
2. When the parents feel the need for help from the professional;
3. At various stages of the child's development; when a crisis is apt to occur;
4. When the child poses problem of adjustment or difficulties in training of management;
5. When there is a change in the child's environment in the home or school;

6. When the parents are in doubt about having another child;
7. When the parent requires suggestions regarding the placement of the child in a special school, in an institution, a training centre etc.;
8. When problems of sex and marriage are involved;
9. When suggestions for suitable vocational placement is needed.

Who should Counsel the Parents

Obviously, he should be a member of the Medico-Socio-Educational team, all of who are involved in the services of the handicapped. Together with their basic professional qualification, training in counselling and guidance, and experience in the field of handicapped is necessary.

In general, the counsellor should be aware of the services and facilities available for the handicapped and should have an understanding of the parents tensions, anxieties and the best way to relieve them.

The Counselling Situation

1. It should provide an opportunity for the parents to express their feelings in a non-threatening interpersonal interaction.
2. The parent should be accepted and respected for what he is.
3. Decisions should be reached by parents rather than the counsellor
4. Parents should determine the direction of the interview.
5. Counsellor and counsellee should be honest in exchanging their views.
6. Genuine interest should be shown towards the child and his parent.
7. Counsellor should be patient.

8. Printed communication that can be understood by parents may be handed out.
9. The efforts made by the parents should be encouraged and appreciated.
10. The initial shock, guilt feelings, frustrations, the effects on the handicapped child's family and the future, should be discussed freely.
11. Objective information to be provided regarding diagnosis, education, social, legal and financial problems.
12. Practical guidance should be given regarding, care, occupation and training of their child.
13. Parents should be apprised of the child's limitations and potentialities to accept reality and to enjoy the smallest progress.

(i) Forms of Counselling

(a) *Counselling of Individual Parents:* In the initial sessions it is preferable to see individual parents-couples rather than groups of parents. In these sessions, either the father or mother or preferably both may attend.

It is better always that both parents attend together for the initial sessions. Otherwise one partner finds a difficulty in conveying the information to the other.

Initial Sessions: Should deal with getting to know the family dynamics. This will enable the counsellor to be able to support the parents after the initial shock, to allay guilt feelings, frustrations on their having the diagnosis of retardation confirmed.

The following sessions will cover the level of the child, his potentialities, his limitations, the etiological factors, leading to the condition overcoming parental anxieties in adjusting to the new situation, decisions regarding management/placement/ training/education of the child. Practical guidance and aid in contacting other agencies for help. It will be necessary at this stage to give courage, comfort and reassurance to indicate to the parents, that they are not alone with their problems.

A couple of sessions, with all the family members may be essential so as to appraise them of the child's condition and to help them to find ways to adjust to it, and also their role in the upbringing of the child.

Number of Sessions, Duration and Frequency: The number of sessions depends on the type of parents, their educational level, their capacity to comprehend, their acceptance, and cooperation.

The sessions may be held either in the afternoons, or in the evenings about one hour per session about three sessions per week initially, gradually reduced to one session per week.

(ii) Counselling During Crisis Situations

Aims and Objectives

1. To minimise the anxiety of the parents.
2. To suggest means and ways to the parent to overcome the crisis situation.

Number of Sessions, Duration and Frequency: As and when the crisis arises—till the parent feels that he/she can cope with the situation.

(iii) Genetic Counselling

Aims and Objectives: Enlightening the parents of the factors responsible for the child's condition; and also the chances of similar child being born again into the family in case the factors responsible were hereditary in nature.

When the Counselling should be given? It should be given when the parent asks whether it is advisable to have another child.

Outcome of Genetic Counselling: The counsellor should not make the decisions; but supply the information and leave the decision to the parents themselves.

(iv) Group Counselling

Aims and Objectives:

1. To enable parents of children with mental retardation to go together to discuss their problems, to give suggestions, to lend mutual emotional support to one another;
2. To realise that there are others who have similar problems;
3. To decrease their fears regarding public attitudes;
4. To give them training in the management of their child;
5. To facilitate them to most parents of children of different age groups, with their children;
6. To provide recreational facilities.

Structure of the Groups:

1. The groups can comprise of both parents, with children of all ages;
2. Groups consisting of only mothers;
3. Groups consisting of all the members of the family;
4. Groups consisting of parents, of similar age group of children.

It would be better to limit the number in the group to 10, the frequency once a week, preferably in the afternoon or evenings to facilitate both parents to attend; the duration about two hours per session.

Functions of the Group:

1. The group may be brought together for purpose of discussion, regarding mutual problems and ways of solving them;
2. The group may be an activity group, when parents engage themselves in playing with the child, or demonstrating an aspect of the training programme, to the other parents. The group may also spend the time during the session by listening to a special lecture

or by seeing a film, on some aspect of mental retardation.

Methods:

1. Discussions;
2. Talk by the specialist or a parent on a particular aspect of mental retardation;
3. Practical demonstrations by the counsellor;
4. Parents practising the training programme;
5. Playing with the child with appropriate toys;
6. Audio-visual aids, pamphlets.

(v) Training Parents through Workshops

Training parents is an extension of counselling incorporated into the training programme.

Aims and Objectives:

1. To train and educate parents to train their children at home;
2. To enable the parents to participate and enjoy the pleasure of training;
3. To make the parent feel that she is an active partner in the training programme;
4. To enable to follow sequentially, the child's development, through various phases at the same time becoming aware of the obstacles and impediments to progress, the causes for these and how to overcome them;
5. To be able to perceive even the smallest improvement or development of behaviour;
6. To know the limitations, potentialities of the child through experience.

Structure of the Groups

Parents of profoundly and severely mentally retarded children.

Parents with mentally retarded children of ages below three years.

Parents with mentally retarded child aged 3-6 years.

The number should not be more than 10 parents in a group, the frequency twice a week, preferably in the evenings, and the duration about 11/2-2 hours per session for 6 weeks.

Procedure

1. Assessment of child.
2. Assessment of parental attitudes.
3. Formation of the group.

Sessions

First Session: Introduction of members, orientation to the purpose of the group.

Second Session-Fourth Session: Brief introduction to a child's normal development, mental retardation and etiology of mental retardation, the management. Talks may be given by different professionals.

Fifth Session: Discussion by the group.

Sixth Session: Discussion of level of each child and planning of training programme according to the level of the child. The parent starts the programme at home.

Seventh Sessions onwards: Discussion of parents regarding the training progress, difficulties etc.

Last two sessions: Discussions, regarding the reassessment made and also further training programme at home.

Follow up and assessment should be made once in two months.

Counselling aims at helping parents to understand and accept their child's problems. It also helps to evaluate and develop plans which are appropriate to the capacity of the mentally retarded individual. So to perform such a duty effectively, a counsellor should have certain skills and characteristics. These includes:

(a) *Dedication:* Dedication and sincerity is the most important and the basic quality of a successful counsellor. This makes the client to develop trust and confidence in him. Otherwise, the client wouldn't reveal or come out freely with all their problems they face with mentally retarded child. Confidential in maintaining the information about the client and the family situation is also an important task of a counsellor. As a counsellor he/she should have an unconditional regard towards the client and he should have an unbiased behaviour.

(b) *Reassurance:* Parents should feel that the counsellor understand them and the problems they face. As a counsellor he has to listen patiently even if the information seems unimportant. But at the same time he should be careful not to give false hopes to the parents. Counsellor should render his service by developing trust in him.

(c) *Skill in Communication:* In the process of counselling, simple language should be used. Technical language should be avoided. This inturn helps the parents to follow, what is communicated. Honest and true information on the child's condition and the facilities available should be conveyed. Final decision regarding management should be left to the choice of the parents.

(d) *Emotional Stability:* Parents get frustrated when the parents learn that their child will not become normal. Sometimes they become aggressive towards counsellor. At that point, as a counsellor he/she should maintain the emotions and he/she should not react adversely to the feelings of the parents. As a counsellor he/she should know that clients are not upset with him but with the situation they are facing and ventilating their feelings. It is the duty of a counsellor to make the parents feel relieved from the anxiety and frustration, they had been lodging for a long time and guide the parents to accept and involve in the rehabilitation programme available for their child. Counselling depends upon the individual needs of the mentally retarded child and his family.

Stages in Parents Counselling

Stage-1: Providing information regarding the condition of mentally retarded child.

(i) Explaining child's actual condition in simple words to the parents.

(ii) Giving false explanation, building false hopes in parents should be avoided

(iii) Providing information and directing parents to get-help from professional for associated conditions like fits, hyperactivity or other secondary handicaps

(iv) Counselling should not be made in a hurry

Stage-2: Developing right attitude towards their mentally retarded child

(i) Beliefs, attitudes and ideas of the parents regarding the causes may be wrong. This is more prone in the case, of mental retardation. Parents believe that their child would become normal in due course of time. In some case parents blame each other for being responsible for the birth of such a child and experience guilty. Some goes for medical, surgical and magical cure for their child's condition. Some parents think that their child is useless and they can't do anything. At this juncture, it is the counsellor who can develop right attitude in a right direction.

(ii) Some parents are overprotective, whereas some parents exhibit rejection towards mentally retarded children. Overprotection is shielding the child from any challenging situation or doing almost everything for the child before child attempt it. This type of action hinders the development of the child whatever capacities the child may have.

At another extreme some parents totally ignores the child and this mentality should be changed by the counsellor.

(iii) Counsellor's another important task is making parents to realize the capabilities and ability of the child. Because some parents expect their child to learn or achieve beyond his abilities.

Stage-3: Involving parents in the training

(i) Many parents think that it is the duty of the practitioners or teachers to train mentally retarded individual. As a counsellor he/she should explain the effectiveness and role of the parents and family members in training mentally retarded children.

(ii) Parents are made aware that only simple step with repeated training is effective when the mentally retarded child learn. Because some parents think that training a mentally retarded child needs specialized skills.

(iii) Mutual support is made developed by the counsellor by arranging frequent meetings among parents of mentally retarded child.

(iv) Helping parents to using demonstrations and observations in training their child.

(v) Involvement of parents in training programme is increased once they view the progress of the child.

Thus a counsellor plays a vital role in the process of training mentally retarded children.

(II) Counselling Peer Group and Community

Better learning takes place when mentally retarded children are trained with their non-handicapped peer group. This process is effectively carried out where there is peer acceptance. To make the peer group to accept the mentally retarded children counsellor should make them to know that the mentally retarded children also like them. They have same feeling, emotions and interest as we have. Positive attitude about mentally retarded children is created by the counsellor.

Community plays a vital role for the development of children with mental retardation. As a counsellor, it is his/her duty to change the community negative attitude into positive one towards mentally retarded. Community thinks that mental retardation in children is due to sin of their parents or the child. This attitude should be changed. Community also possess some false beliefs and practices about causes and treatment. This should be overcomed by the counsellor.

In the process of community counselling, sensitising the community people about the nature of mental retardation, causes and characteristics of mental retardation, the ways and means to prevent mental retardation, and the educational services available for the mentally retarded children should find place. Organizing street plays, dramas, dance and folk cultural programmes on mental retardations, banners, posters and brochures about causes and characteristics of mental retardation, ways of identification and educational treatments available for mental retardation should be included in the community counselling. Jathas and meetings on ways and means to prevent mental retardation and how to handle if there is a mentally retarded children in the community will certainly develop positive attitude in the community about mental retardation. Community counselling plays a vital role to accept the mentally retarded children as one among them. This positive attitude certainly will lead for independence in mentally retarded individual. At the same time, counselling to the mentally retarded individual is also one of the important tasks. These help the children to develop self-confidence, self-esteem and self-reliance. Counselling helps him to be independent as much as possible.

Thus guidance and counselling plays an important part in the process of education for mentally retarded children. To cater this valuable jobs in a right way an individual need intensive training.

Summary

Career education makes education more relevant to the economic and employment realities of the day. Career education is the totality of experiences through which one learns about and prepares to engage in work. Career education has four stage namely—career awareness, career exploration, career preparation and placement. There are three career education model explained in this chapter. They are Clark's school based models, life-centered competency based model and experience based career education model. There are various instructional approaches in career education. Career education is given through academic subjects like mathematics, language arts, and social sciences.

Career Education is a much broader concept that encompasses vocational education. Various vocational placement is available for mentally retarded children. They are open employment, and sheltered workshops.

Parents counselling is an important process in training mentally retarded. Effective counsellor should possess various characteristics like dedication, reassurance, better communication ability and emotionally stable. Parents are counselled at three stages. Providing information regarding the condition of mentally retarded child, developing right attitude towards mentally retarded child and involving parents in the training programme for mentally retarded child. Counselling to the peer group and to the community is also important task in the training process of mentally retarded children.

References

Alberto, P., Troutman, A. (1982) 'Applied Behaviour Analysis for Teachers'. Columbus, Ohio: Charles E. Merrill Publishing Co.

Aman, M.G., Hammer, D. and Rojahn, J. (1993) 'Mental Retardation'. In T.H. Ollendick and M. Hersen (Eds.), *Handbook of Child and Adolescent Assessment*. Boston: Allyn and Bacon.

Atkinson, R.C. (1975) 'Mnemotechnics in Second Language Learning'. *American Psychologist*, 30, 821-28.

Axelrod, S. (1977) 'Behaviour Modification for the Classroom Teacher'. New York: McGraw-Hill Book Co.

Balla, D. and Zigler, E. (1979) 'Personality Development in Retarded Persons'. In N.R. Ellis (Ed.), Handbook of Mental Deficiency: *Psychological Theory and Research*. 2nd Edition. Hillsdale, NJ: Erlbaum.

Bayley, N. (1969) 'Bayley Scales of Infant Development'. New York: Psychological Corporation.

Beck, R. (1977) 'The Need for Adjuntive Services in the Management of Severely and Profoundly Handicapped Individuals: A Review from Primary Care'. In N.G. Haring and L. Brown (Eds.), Teaching the Severely Handicapped, Vol. 2, New York, Grune and Stratton.

Bellezza, F.S. (1981) 'Mnemonic Devices: Classification Characteristics, and Criteria'. Review of Educational Research, 51, 247-75.

Bijou, S.W. (1966) 'A Functional Analysis of Retarded Development'. In N.R. Ellis (Ed.,) International Review of Research in Mental Retardation (Vol. 1, pp. 1-19), New York: Academic Press.

Bill R. Gearheart, James A. DeRuiter, Thomas W. Sileo (1988) 'Teaching Mildly and Moderately Handicapped Students'. Prentice-Hall of India.

Binet, A. and Simon, T. (1905) 'Methods Nouvelles Pourle Diagnostic du niveau Intellectual des anormaux'. L'Annee Psychoogique, 1, 191-244.

Borkowski, J.G and Waschura, P.B. (1974) 'Mediational Processes in the Retarded'. In N.R. Ellis (Ed.), International Review of Research in Mental Retardation, Vol. 7, New York: Academic Press.

Borkowski, J.G. and Cavanaugh, J.C. (1979) 'Maintenance and Generalization of Skills and Strategies by the Retarded'. In N.R. Ellis (Ed.), *Handbook of Mental Deficiency: Psychological Theory and Research.* 2nd Edition, Hillsdale, NJ: Lawrence Erlbaum.

Borkowski, J.G., Peck, V. A. and Damberg, P.R. (1983) 'Attention, Memory and Cognition'. In J.L. Matson and J.A. Mulich (Eds.), Handbook of Mental Retardation. New York: Pergamon Press.

Bray, N.W. (1979) 'Strategy Production in the Retarded'. In N.R. Ellis (Ed.), Handbook of Mental Deficiency: Psychological Theory and Research. 2nd Edition, Hillsdale, NJ: Lawrence Erlbaum.

Bregman, J.D. and Hodapp, R.M. (1991) 'Current Developments in the Understanding of Mental Retardation: Part-I. Biological and Phenomenological Perspectives'. *Journal of American Academy of Child and Adolescent Psychiatry*, 30, 707-719.

Brolin D.E. (1982) 'Vocational Preparation of Persons with Handicaps'. Columbus, OH: Charles E. Merrill.

Brolin, D.E. and Kokaska, C.J. (1979) 'Career Education for Handicapped Children and Youth'. Columbus, OH: Charles E. Merrill.

Brolin, D.E., McKay, D.J. and West, L.W. (1978) 'Trainer's Guide for life Centered Career Education'. Reston, VA: Council for Exceptional Children.

Broman, S., Nichols, P.L., Shaunghnessy, P. and Kennedy, W. (1987) 'Retardation in Young Children: A Developmental Study of Cognitive Deficit'. Hillsdale, NJ: Erlbaum.

Brooks, P.H. and McCauley, C. (1984) 'Cognitive Research in Mental Retardation'. *American Journal of Mental Deficiency*, 88, 479-486.

Brown, A.L. (1974) 'The Role of Strategic Behaviour in Retarded Memory'. In N.R. Ellis (Ed.), International Review of Research in Mental Retardation, Vol. 7, New York: Academic Press.

Brown, R.T. and Alford, N. (1984) 'Ameliorating Attentional Deficits and Concomitant Academic Deficiencies in Learning Disabled Children Through Cognitive Training'. *Journal of Learning Disabilities*, 17, 20-26.

Buzan, T. (1976) 'Use Both Sides of Your Brain'. New York: E.P. Dutton.

Calkins, L.M. (1979) 'Andrea Learns to Make Writing Hard'. Language Arts, 56, 569-76.

Carr, J. (1994) 'Long Term Outcome for People with Down's Syndrome'. *Journal of Child Psychology and Psychiatry*, 35, 425-439.

Clark Denver, G.M. (1979) 'Career Education for the Handicapped Child in the Elementary Classroom'. CO: Love Publishing Co.

Craik, F.I.M. and Tulving, E. (1975) 'Depth of Processing and the Retention of Words in Episodic Memory'. Journal of Experimental Psychology: General, 104, 268-294.

Craik, F.I.M., and Lockhart, R.S. (1972) 'Levels of Processing: A Framework for Memory Research'. Journal of Verbal Learning and Verbal Behaviours, 11, 671-684.

Daigon, Arthur (1982) 'Towards Righting Writing'. Phi Delta Kappan, 64, No. 4, 242-246.

Daniel, P. Hallahan and James M. Kauffman (1991) 'Exceptional Children-Introduction to Special Education'. 5th Ed. Prentice-Hall International Limited, UK, London.

De Ruiter, J.A. and Wansart, W.L. (1982) 'Psychology of Learning Disabilities: Applications and Educational Practice'. Rockville, Md: Aspen Systems Corp.

Deshler, D.D. and Schumaker, J.B. (1983) 'Social Skills of Learning Disabled Adolescents: Characteristics and Intervention. Topics in Learning and Learning Disabilities, 3. 15-23.

Diamond, G.W. and Cohen, H.J. (198) 'AIDS and Developmental Disabilities'. Prevention Update, National Coalition on Prevention of Mental Retardation.

Driskell, J. (1977) 'Mapping the Idea: A Note Taking System'. Paper Presented at the 10th Annual Meeting of the Western College Reading Association, Denver, Mar. 31-Apr. 2.

Erickson, E.H. (1968) 'Identify: Youth and Crisis'. New York: Norton.

Estes, W.K. (1970) 'Learning Theory and Mental Development'. New York: Academic Press.

Fagen, S. and Long, N.J. (1979) 'A Psycho-educational Curriculum Approach to Teaching Self Control'. Behaviour Disorders, 4, 68-82.

Fagen, S., Long, N.J. and Stevens, D.J. (1975) 'Teaching Children Self-control'. Columbus, Ohio: Charles E. Merrill Publishing Co.

Fernald, G. (1943) 'Remedial, Techniques in Basic School Subjects'. New York: McGraw-Hill Book Co.

Finch Jr. A.J. and Spirito, A. (1980) 'Use of Cognitive Training to Change Cognitive Processes'. Exceptional Education Quarterly, Vol. 1, 31-39.

Forrest, E.B. (1981) 'Visual Imagery as an Information Processing Strategy'. *Journal of Learning Disabilities*, 14, 584-86.

Freud, S. (1924) 'The Passing of the Oedipus Complex'. In E. Jones (Ed.), Collected Papers of Sigmund Freud, Vol. 5, New York: Basic Books.

Garwood, S.G. (1983) 'Educating Young Handicapped Children'. 2nd ed. Rock ville, Md.: Aspen Systems Corp.

Gessell, A. (1940) 'Gessell Developmental Schedules'. Cheshire, CT: Nigel Cox.

Gessell, A. and Armatrida, C.S. (1941) 'Developmental Diagnosis'. New York: Hoeber.

Gillberg, C. (1997) 'Practitioner Review: Physical Investigations in Mental Retardation'. *Journal of Child Psychiatry and Psychology* 38, 889-897.

Glasser, W. (1975) 'Reality Therapy: A New Approach to Psychiatry'. New York: Harper and Row Publishers.

Glidden, I.M. (1985) 'Semantic Processing, Semantic Memory, and Recall'. In N.R. Ellis (Ed.), International Review of Research in Mental Retardation, Vol. 13, pp. 247-278, New York: Academic Press.

Glover, J.A., Zimmer, J.W., Filbeck, R.W. and Plake, B.S. (1980) 'Effects of Training Students to Identify the Semantic Base of Prose Materials'. Journal of Applied Behaviour Analysis, 13, 655-67.

Goldstein, A.P. (1981) 'Psychological Skills Training'. Elmsford, N.Y. Pergamon Press.

Goldstein, A.P. and Klein, P. (1980) 'Skill Streaming the Adolescent: A Structured Learning Approach to Teaching Prosocial Skills'. Champaign, Ill: Research Press Co.

Goldstein, A.P., Sprafkin, R.P. and Gershaw, N.J. (1979) 'I Know What's Wrong But Don't Now What To Do About It'. Englewood Cliffs, N.J.: Prentice-Hall.

Grinnel, P.C. and Burris, N.A. (1983) 'Drawing and Writing: The Emerging Graphic Communication Process'. Topics in Learning and Learning Disabilities, 3, 21-32.

Grossman, H. (1983) 'Manual on Terminology and Classification in Mental Retardation'. Revised. Washington, DC: American Association on Mental Deficiency.

Grossman, H.J. (1983) 'Classification in Mental Retardation'. Washington, D.C.: American Association on Mental Deficiency.

Hallahan, D.P. and Sapona, R. (1983) 'Self-monitoring of Attention with Learning Disabled Children: Past Research and Current Issues'. *Journal of Learning Disabilities*, 16, 616-620.

Hayden, A.H. and Edgar, E.B. (1977) 'Identification, Screening and Assessment'. In J.B. Jordan et al. (Eds.), Early Childhood Education for Exceptional Children. Reston, VA: Council for Exceptional Children.

Hayes, D. (1982) 'Handwriting Practice: The Effects of Perceptual Prompts'. *Journal of Education Research*, 75, 169-172.

Hayes, J.R. (1981) 'The Complete Problem Solver'. Philadelphia: Franklin Institute Press.

Heber, R.F. (1961) 'A Manual on Terminology and Classification in Mental Retardation'. Washington, DC: American Association on Mental Deficiency.

Hetherington, E.M. and Parker, R.D. (1986) 'Child Psychology: A Contemporary Viewpoint'. 3rd Edition. New York: McGraw Hill.

Howlin, P., Davies, M. and Udwin, D. (1998) 'Cognitive Functioning in Adults with Williams Syndrome'. *Journal of Child Psychology and Psychiatry*. 39, 183-189.

Hoyt, K.B. (1975) 'An Introduction to Career Education'. A Policy Paper of the U.S. Office of Education. Washington, DC: Office of Education.

Itard, J.M. (1932) 'The Wild Toy of Averyon'. (G. Humpberg and Humpherg, Trans). New York: Appleton-Century-Crofts. (Originally published in 1894).

Iwata, B. and Bailey, J. (1974) 'Reward Versus Cost Token Systems: An Analysis of the Effects on Students and Teacher'. *Journal of Applied Behaviour Analysis*, 7, 567-76.

Jane Mercer (1973) 'Labelling the Mentally Retarded'. Berkeley: University of California Press.

Jones, B.F. and Hall, J.W. (1982) 'School Applications of the Mnemonic Keyword Method as a Study Strategy by Eighth Grades'. *Journal of Educational Psychology*, 74, 230-37.

Justice E.M. (1985) 'Metamory: An Aspect of Metacognition in the Mentally Retarded'. In N.R. Ellis (Ed.), International Review of Research in Mental Retardation, Vol. 13 (pp. 79-107), New York: Academic Press.

Kakalik, J.S., Brewer, G.D., Dougherty, L.A., Fleischauer, P.D., and Genensky, S.M. (1973) 'Services for Handicapped Youth'. (Report to the Department of the Health, Education and Welfare, Washington, DC, Office of the Assistant Secretary for Planning and Evaluation)'. Santa Monica, CA: Rand Corporation.

Kamii, C. (1984) 'Autonomy: The Aim of Education Envisioned by Piaget'. Phi Delta Kapan, 65, 410-15.

Kanner, L. (1964) 'A History of the Care and Study of the Mentally Retarded'. Spring Field, IL: Charles C. Thomas.

Kazdin, A. and Bootzin, R. (1972) 'The Token Economy: An Evaluative Review'. *Journal of Applied Behaviour Analysis*, 5, 343-72.

Keogh, B.K. and Glover, A.T. (1980) 'The Generality and Durability of Cognitive Training Effects'. *Exceptional Education Quarterly* 1, 75-82.

Kirk, S.A., Kliebhan, J.M. and Lerner, J.W. (1978) 'Teaching, Reading to Slow and Disabled Learners'. Boston: Houghton Mifflin Co.

Klatzky, R.L. (1975) 'Human Memory: Structures and Processes'. 2nd Edition, San Francisco: WH. Freeman and Co.

Kneedler, R.D. (1980) 'The Use of Cognitive Training to Change Social Behaviours'. *Exceptional Education Quarterly* I, 65-73.

Kohlberg, L. (1969) 'Stage and Sequence: The Cognitive Developmental Approach to Socialisation'. In D.A. Goslin (Ed.), Handbook of Socialisation Theory and Research. Chicago: Rand McNally.

Kronick, D. (1983) 'Social Development of Learning Disabled Persons: Examining the Effects and Treatments of Inadequate Interpersonal Skills'. San Francisco: Jossey Bass Publishers.

Lahey, B. and Drabman, R. (1981) 'Behaviour Modification in the Classroom'. In W.E. Craighead, A. Kazdin and M. Mahoney, (eds.), Behaviour Modification: Principles, Issues and Application. 2nd ed. Boston: Houghton Mifflin Co.

Larson, C. (1982) 'Personal Communication Regarding the EBCE-MD LD Models, 1981'. Cited in D.E. Brolin, Vocational Preparation of Persons with Handicaps. Columbus, OH: Merrill.

Law, S.G. (1998) 'The Use of Non Word Repetition as a Test of Phonological Memory in Children with Down Syndrome'. *Journal of Child Psychology and Psychiatry*, 39, 1119-1130.

Leahy, R., Balla, D. and Zigler, E. (1982) 'Role Taking, Self-image, and Imitation in Retarded and Non-retarded Individuals'. *American Journal of Mental Retardation*, 92 (5), 472-475.

Levin, J.R. (1981) 'The Mnemonic 80's: Keywords in the Classroom'. *Educational Psychologist*, 16, 65-82.

Levin, J.R., McCormick, C.B., Miller, G.E., Berry, J.K. and Pressley, M. (1982) 'Mnemonic Versus Non-mnemonic Vocabulary—learning Strategies for Children'. *American Educational Research Journal*, 19, 121-36.

Lloyd, J. (1980) 'Academic Instruction and Cognitive Behaviour Modification: The Need for Attack Strategy Training'. Exceptional Education Quarterly, Vol. 1, 53-63.

Lokanadha Reddy, G. and Kusuma, A. (1995) 'Mental Retardation in Children—causes and Prevention'. Balak-*The Quarterly Journal of the Indian Association for Pre-school Education*, Gandhigram Press.

Luckasson, R. et. al. (1992) 'Mental Retardation: Definition, Classification and Systems of Supports'. Washington, DC: American Association on Mental Retardation.

Luftig, R.L. (1988) 'Assessment of the Perceived School Loneliness and Isolation of Mentally Retarded and Non-retarded Students'. *American Journal of Mental Retardation*, 92 (5), 472-475.

MacMillan , D.L. (1982) 'Mental Retardation in School and Society'. 2nd Edition, Boston, Little Brown.

MacMillan, D.L. and Forness, S.R. (1973) 'Behaviour Modification: Savior or Servant's'? In R.K. Eyman, P.E. Meyer and G. Tarian (Eds.), Socio-behaviour Studies in Mental Retardation. Washington, DC: American Association on Mental Deficiency.

Madhavan, T., Manjula Kalyan, Shakila Naidu, Reeta Peshawaria and Jayanthi Narayan (1989) 'Mental Retardation—A Manual for Psychologists'. National Institute for the Mentally Handicapped, Secunderabad.

McGue, M., Bouchard, T.J. Iacono, W.G. and Lyken, D.T. (1993) 'Behavioural Genetics of Cognitive Ability: A Life-span Perspective'. In R. Plomin and G.E. McClean (Eds.) Nature, Nurture and Psychology. Washington, DC: American Psychological Association.

Meichenbaum, D. (1977) 'Cognitive Behaviour Modification'. New York: Plenum Press.

Miller Patricia, H. (1983) 'Theories of Developmental Psychology'. San Francisco: W.H. Freeman and Co.

Morse, W.C. (1971) 'Crises Interventions in School Mental Health and Special Classes for the Disabled'. In N.J. Long, W.C. Morse and R.G. Newman, Eds., Conflict in the Classroom: The Education of Children with Problems. Belmont, Calif: Wadsworth.

Morse, W.C. (1976) 'Worksheet on Life Space Interviewing for Teachers'. In Conflict in the Classroom'. 3rd Edition. Belmont, Calif: Wadsworth.

Mussen, P.H. and Eisenberg-Berg, W. (1977) 'Roots of Caring, Sharing and Helping. San Francisco: W.H. Freeman and Co.

Neisworth, J.T. and Smith, R.M. (1978) 'Retardation: Issues, Assessment and Interventions'. New York: McGraw-Hill Company.

Nihira, K., Foster, R., Shellhaa, M. and Leland, H. (1975) 'AAMD Adaptive Behaviour Scale Manual'. (rev. ed.). Washington, DC: American Association on Mental Deficiency.

O'Leary , D. and O'Leary, S. (1977) 'Classroom Management: The Successful Use of Behaviour Modification'. New York: Pergamon Press.

Pearl, R., Bryan, T. and Donahue, M. (1983) 'Social Behaviours of Learning Disabled: A Review'. Topics in Learning and Learning Disabilities, 3, 1-14.

Piaget, J. (1932, 1965) 'The Moral Judgement of the Child'. London: Routledge and Kegan Paul.

Plomin, R., De Fries , J.C. and McClearn, G.E. (1990) 'Behavioural Genetics: A Primer'. 2nd Edition, New York: W.H. Freeman and Company.

Polloway, E.A., Patton, J.R. and Cohen, S.B. (1981) 'Written Language for Mildly Handicapped Students'. *Focus on Exceptional Children*, 14, No. 3, 1-16.

Raven, J.C., Court, J.H. and Raven, J. (1985) 'A Manual for Raven's Progressive Matrices and Vocabulary Scales'. London: HK. Lewis.

Reddy, G.L. (2004) 'Awareness, Attitude and Competencies Required for Special and Normal School Teachers in Dealing Children with Disabilities'. Research Project Report, Department of Education, Alagappa University, Karaikudi.

Redl, F. (1959) 'The Concept of Life Space Interview'. *American Journal of Orthopsychiatry*, 29, 1-18.

Reid, D.K. and Hresko, W.P. (1981) 'A Cognitive Approach to Learning Disabilities'. New York: McGraw Hill Book Co.

Rosenthal, T. and Bandura, A. (1978) 'Psychological Modelling: Theory and practice'. N.S. Garfield and A. Bergin, eds., Handbook of Psychotherapy and Behaviour Change. New York: John Wiley and Sons.

Rossen, M., Klima, E.S., Bellugi, U., Bihrle, A. and Jones, W. (1996) 'Interaction Between Language and Cognition: Evidence from Williams syndrome'. In J.H. Beitchman, N.J. Cohen, M.M. Konstantareas and R. Tannock (Eds.), Language, Learning and Behaviour Disorders. New York: Cambridge University Press.

Rubinstein, A. (1989) 'Background, Epidemiology and Impact of HIV Infection in Children'. *Mental Retardation*, 27(4), 209-211.

Salvia, J. (1978) 'Perspective on the Nature of Retardation'. In J.T. Neisworth and R.M. Smith (Eds.), Retardation: Issues, Assessment and Intervention. New York: McGraw Hill, 27-47.

Schnell, T.R. and Rocchi, D.J. (1974) 'A Study of the Relative Effectiveness of Various Underlining Strategies on Reading Comprehension'. Paper Presented At the 18th Annual Meeting of the College Reading Association, Bethesda, Md., Oct. 31-Nov.2.

Schultz, E.E., Jr. (1983) 'Depth of Processing by Mentally Retarded and MA—matched Non-retarded Individual. *American Journal of Mental Deficiency*, 88, 307-313.

Scott, K.C. and Carran, D.T. (1987) 'The Epidemiology and Prevention of Mental Retardation'. American Psychologist Association, 42, 801-804.

Scott, S. (1994) 'Mental Retardation'. In M. Rutter E. Taylor and L. Hersov (Eds.), Child and Adolescent Psychiatry—Modern Approaches. Cambridge, M.A.: Blackwell.

Shriberg, L.K., Levin, J.R., McCormick, C.B. and Pressley, M. (1982) 'Learning About 'Famous' People Via the Keyword'. *Journal of Educational Psychology*, 74, 238-47.

Simonff, E., Bolton, P. and Rutter, M. (1996) 'Mental Retardation: Genetic Findings, Clinical Implications and Research Agenda'. *Journal of Child Psychology and Psychiatry*, 37, 259-280.

Singh, N.N., Oswald, D.P. and Ellis, C.R. (1998) 'Mental Retardation'. In T.H. Ollendick and M. Hersen (Eds.), Handbook of Child Psychopathology. New York: Plenum Press.

Skeels, H.M. (1966) 'Adult Status of Children with Contrasting Early Life Experiences: A follow-up Study'. Monographs of the Society for Research in Child Development, 31, 39, Serial No. 105.

Skeels, H.M. and Dye, H.B. (1939) 'A Study of the Effects of Differential Stimulation on Mentally Retarded Children'. Proceedings and Addresses of the American Association on Mental Deficiency., 44 (1), 114-136.

Smith, F. (1978) 'Reading without Nonsense'. New York: Teachers College Press.

Sparrow, S.S., Balla, D.A. and Cicchetti, D.V. (1984) 'Vineland Adaptive Behaviour Scales: Expanded form Manual'. Circle Pines, MN: American Guidance Service.

State, M.W., King, B.H. and Dykens, E. (1997) 'Mental Retardation: A Review of the Past 10 years—Part-II'. *Journal of the American Academy of Child and Adolescent Psychiatry*, 36, 1664-1671.

Sternberg, R.J. and Spear, I.C. (1985) 'A Triarchic Theory of Mental Retardation'. In N.R. Ellis (Ed.), International Review of Research in Mental Retardation, Vol. 13 (pp. 301-326), New York: Academic Press.

Sulzer, B., Mayer, R. (1972) 'Behaviour Personnel Modification Procedures for School Personnel'. New York: Holt, Rinehart and Winston.

Sykes, D., Douglas, V., Morgenstern, G. (1973) 'Sustained Attention in Hyperactive Children'. *Journal of Child Psychology and Psychiatry*. 14, 213-20.

Szymanski, L.S. and Kaplan, L.C. (1991) 'Mental Retardation'. In J.M. Wiener (Ed.), Textbook of Child and Adolescent Psychiatry. Washington, DC: American Psychiatric Association.

Thompson, L.A. (1997) 'Behavioural Genetics and the Classification of Mental Retardation'. In W.E., Machean (Ed.), *Ellis' Handbook of Mental Deficiency, Psychological Theory and Research*. Mahwah, NJ: Lawrence Erlbaum.

Torgesen, J.K. (1982) 'The Learning Disable Child As An Inactive Learners: Educational Implications'. Topics in Learning and Learning Disabilities, 2, 45-52.

Tredgold, (1970) 'Mental Retardation'. (11th Ed.), London, Bailliere, p.7.

Uday Shankar (1984) 'Exceptional Children'. Sterling Publishers, New Delhi.

Ullman, L. and Krasner, L. (1965) 'Case Studies in Behaviour Modification'. New York: Holt, Rinehart and Winston.

Whitman, T.L., O'Callaghan, M. and Sommer, K. (1997) 'Emotion and Retardation'. In W.E. MacLean (Ed.), Ellis' Handbook of Mental Deficiency, Psychological Theory and Research. Mahwah, NJ: Lawrence Erlbaum.

William H. Berdine and A. Edward Blackhurst (1985) 'An Introduction to Special Education'. 2nd Edition, Little Brown and Company, Boston.

Zane, T., Walls, R.T. and Thvedt, J.E. (1981) 'Prompting and Fading Guidance Procedures: Their Effect on Chaining and Whole Task Teaching Strategies'. Education and Training of the Mentally Retarded, 16, 125-35.

Zeamon, D. and House, B.J. (1963) 'The Role of Attention in Retarded Discrimination Learning'. In N.R. Ellis (Ed.), *Handbook of Mental Deficiency*. New York: McGraw Hill.

Zetlin, A.G., Murtaugh, M. (1988) 'Friendship Patterns of Mildly Handicapped and Non Handicapped High School Students'. *American Journal of Mental Retardation,* 92 (5), 447-454.

Zigler, E. and Balla, D. (1982) 'Introduction: The developmental Approach to Mental Retardation'. In E. Zigler and D. Balla (Eds.), Mental Retardation: The Developmental Difference Controversy, (pp. 3-8), Hillsdale, NJ: Erlbaum.

Appendix—I

Gessel Developmental Schedules

The Gessel Developmental Schedules (GDS) represent a standardized procedure for observing and evaluating the course of development in child's daily life. It consists of selected items for assessing maturity in infants and pre-school children in the following four major developmental areas.

1. *Motor Development:* Includes both gross bodily control and finer motor coordination like head balance, postural reactions and locomotion.
2. *Adaptive Behaviour:* Includes perceptual, orientational, manual and verbal adjustments, which reflect the child's capacity to initiate and profit from past experience.
3. *Language Development:* Includes all means of communication such as face expression, gestures, postural movements and vocalizations.
4. *Personal-Social Behaviour:* Includes the child's personal reactions to other play behaviour, social smile, feeding and toilet training.

GDS provides an estimate of Developmental Age (DA) and Developmental Quotient (DQ). It is a useful tool in developmental diagnosis and identification of behavioural abnormalities and mental retardation. GDS can be used for the age range of 1-72 months.

Data on GDS items should be obtained through direct observation of child's responses and supplemented by information gathered from the mother.

Any item on the Developmental Schedule if adequately performed by the child, should be checked with a right (✓) sign. A wrong (x) sign should be used whenever the child fails to perform. In scoring a child's performance developmental examination, several adjacent age levels should be rated under the aggregate of signs changes to an aggregate of x signs. The estimate developmental status is based on the distribution of right and wrong signs.

Find out overall DA and the DA for 'each of the four developmental are Compute DQ by dividing DA and CA and multiplying by 100. Add all DAs and compute the average to obtain overall DQ.

GESSEL DEVELOPMENTAL SCHEDULES RECORD FORM

1.	Name of the child	5.	Sex
2.	Father's name	6.	Date of birth
3.	Mother's name		Year____month_____day___
4.	Date	7.	Age of the child
			Years____ months____days___

RESULTS

Developmental Levels

S. No.	*Developmental Areas*	*DA*	*DQ*
1.	Motor Development		
2.	Adaptive Behaviour		
3.	Language Development		
4.	Personal-Social Behaviour		

Overall Developmental Age (DA):

Overall Developmental Quotient (DQ) = $\frac{DA}{CA} \times 100$:

Remarks

Signature of the Psychologist

GESSEL DEVELOPMENTAL TEST MATERIALS

GESSEL DEVELOPMENTAL SCHEDULES
MOTOR

Items	*4 Weeks*	*16 Weeks*	*28 Weeks*	*40 Weeks*	*12 Months*
SUPINE	Side position head predominates	Mid position head predominates	Lifts head		
	Tonic-neck-reflex posture predominate	Symmetrical postures predominates			
	Both hands fisted	Hands engage			
	Rolls partway to side	Fingers, scratches, clutches			
	Head droops, ventral suspension				
	Placement head rotates				
PRONE	Lifts head momentarily to Zone-1	Head in Zone-III sustained			
	Crawling movements	Legs extended or semi extended		Creeps	
		Verge of rolling			
SITTING	Head predominately sags	Head steady, set forward	Briefly leans forward on hands	Goes to prone	
			Erect momentarily	Indefinitely steady	

(Contd...)

Items	*4 Weeks*	*16 Weeks*	*28 Weeks*	*40 Weeks*	*12 Month*
STANDING			Sustains large fraction of weight Bounces actively	Pulls to feet at rail	
WALKS					Needs only one hand held
RATTLE	Hand clenches on contact				
D. RING		Retains			
RING-STRING				Plucks string easily	
CUBE			Radial palmer grasp	Crude release	
PELET			Rakes, contacts	Grasps promptly Inferior pincer grasp	

GESSEL DEVELOPMENTAL SCHEDULES
ADAPTIVE

Items	*4 Weeks*	*16 Weeks*	*28 Weeks*	*40 Weeks*	*12 Months*
RATTLE	Drop immediately		Shakes definitely		
D.RING/ RATTLE	Regards line vision only	Regards immediately Regards in head			
D. RING	Follows to midline	Free hand to midline To mouth			
D.RING/ RATTLE/ CUBE/CUP		Arms activate			
D.RING/ CUBE			Transfers		
BELL (RINGING)	Attends, activity diminishes				
BELL			Bangs Transfers adeptly Retains	Grasps by handle Sponteneously waves or shakes	
BELL/ RATTLE			One hand approach and grasp		

(Contd...)

Items	*4 Weeks*	*16 Weeks*	*28 Weeks*	*40 Weeks*	*12 Months*
CUBE/CUP		Looks from hand to object			
CUBE			Hold one, grasps another Holds two, more momentarily	Match two cubes	(Demonstration) tries tower, fails
CUP & CUBE				Touches in cube in cup	Release one cube in cup
PELLET				Index finger approach	
PELLETE IN BOTTLE		Regards		Regards pellet if drops out	
POLLETE & BOTTLE				Approaches pellet first Grasps pellet	Tries to insert, releases, fails
RING-STRING					Dangles ring by string
FORM BORAD					Looks selectively at round hole

GESSEL DEVELOPMENTAL SCHEDULES
LANGUAGE

Items	*4 Weeks*	*16 Weeks*	*28 Weeks*	*40 Weeks*	*12 Months*
EXPRESSION	Impassive face Vague, starey & indirect regard	Excites, breathes heavily, strains			
VOCALIZATION	Small throaty noises	Laughs aloud	Crying (m-m-m) Pollysyllabic vowel sounds	Dada and Mama One word	Two words
COMPREHENSION					Gives a toy on request

GESSEL DEVELOPMENTAL SCHEDULES
PERSONAL-SOCIAL

Items	*4 Weeks*	*16 Weeks*	*28 Weeks*	*40 Weeks*	*12 Months*
SOCIAL	Regards examiner's face activity diminishes	Spontaneous social smile Vocalizes or smiles pulled to sit		Waves bye-bye or equivalent	
FEEDING	Require night feedings	Anticipates on sight of foods Sits propped 10-15 minutes	Takes semi-solid or solids well		
PLAY		Hand play, mutual fingering Pulls dress over face	With feet to mouth		
MIRROR			Reaches, pats image		Ball to mirror
RING-STRING			Fusses or abandons effort		
DRESSING					Co- operates in dressing

GESELL DEVELOPMENTAL SCHEDULES

MOTOR

Items	*15 Months*	*18 Months*	*21 Months*	*24 Months*	*30 Months*	*36 Months*	*42 Months*	*48 Months*	*54 Months*	*60 Months*	*72 Months*
STANDING					Tries to stand on 1 foot	Stands on 1 foot mom balance	Stands on 1 foot for 2 sec	Stands on 1 foot 4-8 sec		Stands on 1 foot more than 8 sec	Stands on each foot alt eyes closed
WALKING & RUNNING	Has discarded creeping		Squats in play								
	Walks few steps, starts & stops	Walks fast, runs stiffly (F)		Runs without falling	Walks on tiptoe on demonst ration						
	Falls by collapse (F)	Seldom falls									
SKIPS								Skips on 1 foot	Hops on 1 foot	Skips using feet alternati- vely	

(Contd...)

Items	*15 Months*	*18 Months*	*21 Months*	*24 Months*	*30 Months*	*36 Months*	*42 Months*	*48 Months*	*54 Months*	*60 Months*	*72 Months*
JUMPS					Jumps with both feet	Jumps from bottom stair		Jumps running or broad jump			Jumps from ht. 12" landing on toes only
STAIRS	Creeps up full flight	Walks up 1 hand held	Walks down, hand held	Walks up & down alone		Alternate feet going up		Walks down, a foot to a step			
		Up & down unassisted any method	Walks up, holding rail								
WALKING BOARD							Walks on with both feet	Walks 6 cms. board, touching ground once to balance		Walks 6 cms board with stepping off	Walks length of 4 cms board
CHAIR		Seats self Climbs into	Gets down no help								

(Contd...)

Item	*15 Months*	*18 Months*	*21 Months*	*24 Months*	*30 Months*	*36 Months*	*42 Months*	*48 Months*	*54 Months*	*60 Months*	*72 Months*
CUBES	Tower of 5		Tower of 5-6	Tower of 6-7	Tower of 8						
PELLET BOTTLE	Inserts in bottle					10 in bottle (30 sec)		10 in bottle (25 sec)	(20 sec)	10 in bottle	
BOOK	Helps turn pages	Turns pages 2-3 at a time		Turns pages singly							
PAPER			Folds once imitatively								
BALL		Hurls						Throws overhead			Advanced throwing
LARGE BALL		Walks into (F)	Kicks on demost-ration	Kicks							
DRAWING					Holds crayon by fingers		Traces diamond		Traces cross		Copies diamond

GESELL DEVELOPMENTAL SCHEDULES
ADAPTIVE

Items	*15 Months*	*18 Months*	*21 Months*	*24 Months*	*30 Months*	*36 Months*	*42 Months*	*48 Months*	*54 Months*	*60 Months*	*72 Months*
CUBES	Tower of 2	Tower of 3-4	Tower of 5-6	Tower of 6-7	Tower of 8	Tower of 9 (10 on 3 trails)					
			Imitates pushing train	Aligns-2 or more train	Adds chimney	Imitates bridge	Builds bridge from model	Imitates gate	Makes gate from model	Builds 2 steps	Build 3 steps
CUP & CUBES	6 in & out of cup (F)	10 in cup									
PELLET & BOTTLE		Dumps respons-ively				10 in bottle (30 sec.)		10 in bottle (25 sec.)		10 in bottle (20 sec.)	
DRAWING		Scribbles sponta-neously									
STROKE	Incipient imitation stroke	Makes stroke imitatively		Imitates vertical stroke	Imitates vertical & horizontal						
				Imitates circular stroke	2 or more strokes for cross (F)	Imitates cross					

(Contd...)

Items	*15 Months*	*18 Months*	*21 Months*	*24 Months*	*30 Months*	*36 Months*	*42 Months*	*48 Months*	*54 Months*	*60 Months*	*72 Months*
COPIES						Copies circle		Copies cross	Copies square	Copies triangle	Copies diamond
										Rectangle with diagonals	
COLOUR FORMS					Places-1	Places-2					
GEOMETRIC FORMS						Points to 4	Points to 6	Points to 8	Points to 9 to 10		
MISSING PARTS								1 correct	2 correct		All correct
									Makes aesthetic compari-son		
DIGIT					Repeats 2, 1 or 3 trials	Repeats 3, 1 of trials	Repeats 3, 2 of trials		Repeats 4, 1 of 3 trials		4 correct 2 of 3 trials
COUNTS								Pointing 3 objects	4 objects	10 objects	
										12objects	

(Contd...)

Items	*15 Months*	*18 Months*	*21 Months*	*24 Months*	*30 Months*	*36 Months*	*42 Months*	*48 Months*	*54 Months*	*60 Months*	*72 Months*
										Gives correct number of fingers, separate hands	Correct number of fingers single hand & total
											Adds & sibstracts within five
OWN DRAWING						Names own drawing		Man with 2 parts		Man with body, arms, legs, feet, nose,, mouth, eyes	Man-neck, hands on arms clothes
											Man's legs are 2 dimensional
INCOMPLETE MAN						Names		Add 3 parts		Add 7 parts	Add 9 parts
BUBBLES								One bubble	3 bubbles	1, 2, 3, 4 bubbles	

(Contd...)

Items	*15 Months*	*18 Months*	*21 Months*	*24 Months*	*30 Months*	*36 Months*	*42 Months*	*48 Months*	*54 Months*	*60 Months*	*72 Months*
FORM BOARD	Places round block	Piles 3(F)	Places 2/3	Places blocks on board separately (F)	Places 3 blocks on presen-tation						
	Adapts round block			Adapts in 4 trials	Adapts repaatedly, error (F)	Adapts no error or correction or error					
PERFOR-MANCE			Inserts corner of square (F) Retrieves ball from	Inserts square							
PAPER			Folds once imitati-vely					Folds & creases 3 times demons-tration			
WEIGHTS							Gives heavy block (2 of 3 trials)	Selects heavier (3 of 3 trials)		5 weight 1 error	5 weights no error
SENTE-NCES				Repeats 3-4 syllables		Repeats 6-7 syllables		Repeats 1 of 3 (12, 13 syllables)			

GESELL DEVELOPMENTAL SCHEDULES
LANGUAGE

Items	*15 Months*	*18 Months*	*21 Months*	*24 Months*	*30 Months*	*36 Months*	*42 Months*	*48 Months*	*54 Months*	*60 Months*	*72 Months*
VOCAB-ULARY	4-6 words names	10 words including names	20 words								
SPEECH	Uses jargon		2-3 words spontan-eously	Discarded jargon		Users plurals					
				3-word sentences							
				uses I, me, you							
NAME & SEX					Full name	Tells sex					
BOOK	Pats picture (F)	Looks selectively				Gives action					
PICTURE						Enumer-ates 3 objects				Describes 2 of 3	
PICTURE CARDS	Points Dog/ Shoe	Names/ points one		Names 3/ more	Names 5	Names 8	Names all				
				Identifies 5/more	Identifies 7						

(Contd...)

Items	15 Months	18 Months	21 Months	24 Months	30 Months	36 Months	42 Months	48 Months	54 Months	60 Months	72 Months
COLOUR CARDS								Names 1		Names colours	
BALL		2 Directors	3 Directors	4 Directors							
TEST OBJECTS		Names ball		Names 2	Gives use					Names 5 paise 10 paise 25 paise	
COMPRE-HENSION						A: answers one	A: answers two		B: 1 correct	B: 2 correct	
DIREC-TION						Obeys 2 preposi-tions	Obeys 3 preposi-tions	Obeys 4 proposi-tions		3 Commi-ssions	
ACTION AGENT						7 Correct	9 Correct	13 Correct	14 Correct	15 Correct	
DEFINI-TION									Uses: 4 correct (F)		

GESELL DEVELOPMNTAL SCHEDULES
PERSONAL-SOCIAL

Items	*15 Months*	*18 Months*	*21 Months*	*24 Months*	*30 Months*	*36 Months*	*42 Months*	*48 Months*	*54 Months*	*60 Months*	*72 Months*
FEEDING	Discarded bottles	Party self feeding spilling				Self feeding with little spilling					
	Inhibits grasp of dish	Hands empty dish	Handles glass, lifts, drinks, replaces			Pours well from pitcher					
	Partial regulation	Regulated day time		Dry at night if taken up							
TOILET	Indicates wet under-wears			Verbalizes toilet needs							
	Bowel control										

(Contd...)

Items	15 Months	18 Months	21 Months	24 Months	30 Months	36 Months	42 Months	48 Months	54 Months	60 Months	72 Months
DRESSING							Washes & dries hands or faces	Brushes teeth			
				Pulls on simple garments		unbuttons		Dresses or undresses if supervi-sed		Dresses undresses without assistance	
								Disti-nguishes front & back of clothes			
	Says 'ta ta' or equival-ent		Echoes 2/more last words	Refers to self by name	Refers to self by pronoun	Asks question Rhetori-cally			Calls attent-ion to own perfor-mance	Asks meaning of words	Recites numbers up to thirties
COMMUN-ICATION	Indicates wants		Asks for food, drink toilet	Verbalizes immediate experience	Repetiti-veness in speech	Knows a few rhymes			Relates fanciful stories		Knows right left complete reversal
			Pulls person to show	Compreh-ension & asks for another		Unders-tands taking turns			Boses & criti-cizes others	Diffe-rentiates A.M. & P.M.	

(Contd...)

Items	*15 Months*	*18 Months*	*21 Months*	*24 Months*	*30 Months*	*36 Months*	*42 Months*	*48 Months*	*54 Months*	*60 Months*	*72 Months*
PLAY	Shows or offer toys	Pulls a toy		Hands full cup of cubes to E	Pushes a toy with good force						
	Castes objects playfully	Carries or hugs doll		Plays with domestic mimicry	Helps put things away			Building with blocks		Can print a few letters	
				Parallel play predominates	Carry breakable objects		Associative group play	Plays co-operatively with other children	Shows off dramatically	Dresses up in grown-ups clothes	
DEVELOP MENTAL DETACHMENT								Goes on errands outside home			
								Tends to go out of bounds			

Appendix—II
Senguin form Board Test

Instruction for Administration

The board 's position is so placed that the star is toward the examiner. With the subject watching, the ten pieces are stacked in three piles, starting with the rectangle, in the order shown by the numbers below:

	Examiners Left	*Middle*	*Examiners Right*
Top	Hexagon (3)	Triangle (7)	Diamond (10)
	Oval (2)	Cross (6)	Circle (9)
		Square (5)	
Bottom	Rectangle (1)	Half-Circle (4)	Star (8)

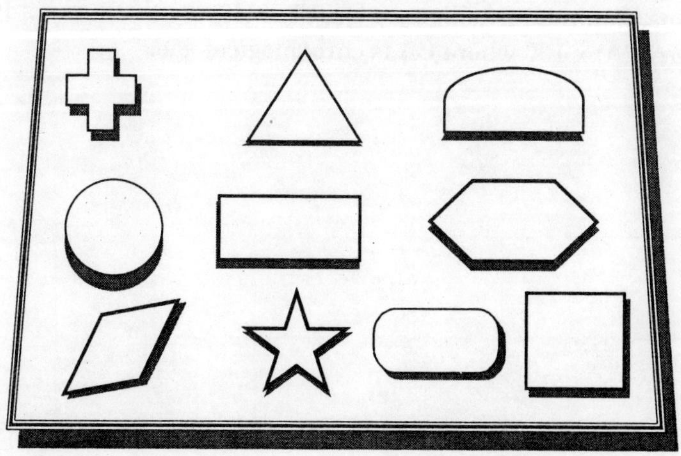

For the child with proper hearing say, "PUT THESE BACK AS FAST AS YOU CAN, READY, GO." Start the stop the watch when you give the command. Count any fraction of a second as a whole second. If any block is left partly outside, resting on the edge instead of fitting into the recess, do not record the time but treat trial as incomplete. Call the subject's attention to the fact that the block or blocks were not complete in place.

For the deaf subject indicate with a gesture that the blocks are all to go back in their places. Use any manual sign for fast with which he is familiar.

The examiner should stack blocks rapidly, but without any suggestion of nervous haste; memorize the bottom to top order; to avoid any hesitation. Say nothing during the progress of a trial.

Make sure that the subject does not start before the signal is given.

The test consists of three trials, including any trial marked incomplete.

The score is the shortest time in seconds out of the three trials.

Convert the score into mental age (MA) be referring to the norms. Compute Intelligence Quotient (IQ) by the formula IQ = (MA/CA) x 100 where CA is chronological age.

NORMS FOR SEGUIN FORM BOARD TEST

Mental age	*3.5*	*4*	*4.5*	*5*	*5.5*	*6*	*6.5*	*7*	*7.5*	*8*	*8.5*	*9*	*9.5*
Shortest of three trials (seconds)	56	46	40	35	31	27	25	23	21.5	20	19	18.5	17.5
Total of three trials (seconds)	216	161	133	125	114	105	98	90	83	77	72	68	64

Mental age	*10*	*10.5*	*11*	*11.5*	*12*	*12.5*	*13*	*13.5*	*14*	*14.5*	*15*	*16*	*17*	*18*	*19*	*20*
Shortest of three trials (seconds)	16.5	16	15	14.5	14	13.5	13	12.5	12.5	12	12	11.5	11	10.5	10.5	10
Total of three trials (seconds)	61	58	55	52	49	46	43	41	39	37	36	35	35	34	34	34

Appendix—III

Development Screening Test

(Bharatraj)

		M	*D*
	birth cry present*		13
	equal bilateral movements		26
	responds to bell		39
	vocalises sounds*		52
	smiles spontaneously		65
	eyes follow moving object		78
3 M	head steady		90
	reaches for objects		15
	laugh aloud*		30
	recognises mother		45
	vocalises for pleasure/babbles*		60
	carried objects to mouth		75
6M	rolls over		90
	imitates speech sounds*		23
	sits by self		46
	thumb finger grasp		68
9M	shows curiosity		90
	says 3 words, 'dada', 'mama' etc.*		23
	stands alone well		46

		M	*D*
1Y	co-operates for dressing		90
	many intelligible words*	1	15
	walks, runs well	3	
	indicates wants	4	15
1Y	Scribbles spontaneously	6	
	Says sentences of two or three words*	1	15
	points out objects in pictures	3	
	shows body parts	4	15
2Y	participate in play	6	
	copies 0	2	
	relates experiences*	4	15
	knows names, uses of common objects	6	
	takes food by self	10	
3Y	toilet control present	12	
	buttons up	2	12
	comprehends 'hunger', 'cold'*	4	24
	plays co-operatively with children	7	6
	repeats 3 digits*	9	18

(Contd...)

		M	D
4Y	tells stories*	12	
	defines words*	2	
	makes simple drawings	4	
	dresses with no supervision	6	
	describes actions in pictures*	8	
	gives sensible answers to questions	10	
5Y	goes about neighbourhood	12	
	Can name primary colour	2	12
	Plays games governed by rules	4	24
	Writes simple words*	7	6
	Gains admission to school	9	18
6Y	Enjoys constructive play	12	
	Adapts to home, school	2	12
	Tells differences of objects	4	24
	Spells, reads, writes simple words	7	6
	Enjoys group play	9	18
7Y	Knows comparative value of coins	12	
	Combs hair by self	3	
	Makes small purchase	6	
	Competition in school/play	9	
8Y	Tells time	12	
	Tells day, Months, year*	2	
	Reads own initiative*	4	
	Recognises property rights	6	
	Favourite of fairy tales*	8	
	Muscle coordination games (marbles)	10	

		M	D
9Y	Bathes self unaided	12	
	Cooperatives keenly with companions	2	12
	Has various hobbies, collections	4	24
	Goes about town freely	7	6
	Sex differences in play become marked	9	18
10Y	Can stay away from home	12	
	Writes occasional short letters*	3	
	Comprehends social situations	6	
	Physical feats liked	9	
11Y	Able to discuss problems*	12	
	Enjoys books, newspapers, magazines*	4	
	More independent in spending	8	
12Y	Capable of self criticism	12	
	Shows foresight, planning, judgement	2	12
	Learns from experience	4	24
	Plays difficult games	7	6
	Instead in dressing up	9	18
13Y	Understands abstract ideas (Justice)	12	
	Makes sensible plans for future (job)	4	24
	Follows current events*	9	18
	Buys own clothing 1Y	2	12
	Systematics own work 1Y	7	6
15Y	Purchases for others 2Y		

Appendix—IV

Vineland Social Maturity Scale

Indian Adaptation by Dr. A.J. Malin

The Vineland Social Maturity Scale (VSMS) measures the differential social capacities of an individual. It provides an estimate of Social Age (SA) and Social Quotient (SQ), and shows high correlation (0.80) with intelligence. It is designed to measure social maturation in eight social areas: Self-help General (SHG), Self-help Eating (SHE), Self-help Dressing (SHD), Self direction (SD), Occupation (OCC), Communication (COM), Locomotion (LOM), and Socialization (SOC). The scale consists of 89 test items grouped into year levels. For details of the complete VSMS one should refer to VSMS manual. VSMS can be used for the age group of 0-15 years.

The examiner should collect information on VSMS test items regarding child's abilities through direct observation and supplement it by interviewing the mother.

Recording

Use Record Sheet for noting the child's responses. Mark the item pass (✓) if the child is able to perform correct and fail (x) if otherwise. Half credits may be given if it can be presumed that the child could have passed the item if the opportunity was present. These half credits receive full credit if they lie between two passed items.

Scoring

Add up passed scores (full and half). Find out the Social Age (SA) from Appendix II of VSMS manual. Compute Social Quotient (SQ) by dividing SA by CA and multiplying by 100.

Assess maturity levels both in terms of SA and SQ for each of the eight social areas by referring VSMS norms and enter in the columns of social maturity constellation record.

VINELAND SOCIAL MATURITY SCALE RECORD SHEET

S.No.	*Test Items*
	0-1 Year
1.	"Crows", Laugh
2.	Balance head
3.	Grasps objects within reach
4.	Reaches for familiar persons
5.	Rolls over, (unassisted)
6.	Reaches for nearby objects
7.	Occupies self-upright
8.	Sits unsupported
9.	Pulls self upright
10.	"Talks", imitates sounds
11.	Drinks from cup or glass assisted
12.	Moves about on floor (creeping, crawling)
13.	Grasps with thumb and finger
14.	Demands personal attention
15.	Stands alone
16.	Does not drool
17.	Follows simple instructions
	1-2 Years
18.	Walks about room unattended
19.	Marks with pencil or crayon or chalk
20.	Masticates (chews) solid or semi-solid food
21.	Pulls off clothes
22.	Transfers objects
23.	Overcomes simple obstacles
24.	Fetches or carries familiar objects
25.	Drinks from cup or glass
26.	Walks without support
27.	Plays with other children
28.	Eats with own hands (biscuits, bread, etc.)
29.	Goes about hours or yard
30.	Discriminates edible substances from non-edibles
31.	Uses names of familiar objects
32.	Walks upstairs unassisted
33.	Unwraps sweets, chocolates
34.	Talks in short sentences
	2-3 Years
35.	Signals to go to toilet
36.	Initiates own play activities
37.	Removes shirt or frock if unbuttond
38.	Eats with spoon/hands (food)
39.	Gets drink (water) unassisted
40.	Dries own hands
41.	Avoids simple hazards
42.	Puts on short or frock unassisted (need not button)
43.	Can do paper folding
44.	Relates experience
	3-4 Years
45.	Walks downstairs, one step at a time
46.	Plays co-operatively at kindergarten level.
47.	Buttons shirt or frock
48.	Helps at little household tasks
49.	"Performs" for others
50.	Washes hands unaided
	4-5 Years
51.	Cares for self at toilet
52.	Washes face unassisted
53.	Goes about neighbourhood unattended

(Contd...)

S.No.	Test Items
54.	Dresses self except for trying
55.	Uses pencil or crayon or chalk for drawing
56.	Plays competitive exercise games
	5-6 Years
57.	Uses hoops, flies kites, or uses knife
58.	Prints (writes) simple words
59.	Plays simple games which require talking turns
60.	Is trusted with money
61.	Goes to school unattended
	6-7 Years
62.	Mixex rice "properly unassisted
63.	Uses pencil or chalk for waiting
64.	Bathes self assisted
65.	Goes to bed unassisted
	7-8 Years
66.	Can differentiate betweween AM & PM
67.	Helps himself during meals
68.	Understands and keeps family secrets
69.	Participants in pre-adole-scent
70.	Combs or bruses hair
	8-9 Years
71.	Uses tools or utensils
72.	Does routine household tasks
73.	Reads on own initiative
74.	Bathes self unaided
	9-10 Years
75.	Cares for self at meals
76.	Makes minor purchase
77.	Goes about home town freely
	10-11 Years
78.	Distinguishes between friends any play mates
79.	Makes independent choice of shops
80.	Does small remunerative work; makes articles
81.	Follows local current events
	11-12 Years
82.	Does simple creative work
83.	Is left to care for self or others
84.	Enjoys reading books, newspapers and magazines
	12-15 Years
85.	Plays difficult games
86.	Exercises complete care of dress
87.	Buys own clothing accessories
88.	Engages of adolescent group activities
89.	Performs responsible routine chores

VINELAND SOCIAL MATURITY SCALE

Explanation of Some Items

1. Vocalizes inarticulately (other than crying or fretting). Spontaneously gargles or coos. Laughs spontaneously or when simulated.
6. Attempts to obtain nearby but beyond reach
7. Plays with rattle or simple objects for quarter hour or longer without need of attention.
14. Indicates desire to be "Talked" to or beyond mere handling, or care for physical needs.
16. Has established control of saliva so that mouth or chin does not require wiping except while eating.
17. Comes when called, points to particular objects in pictures when asked; in general cooperates on verbal request in very simple activities.
22. Pours from one vessel to another without messing; removes, transfers, or replaces objects in somewhat purposeful manner.
23. Opens closed doors; climbs up on chair; uses stool for reaching; removes simple impediments.
26. Walks by pushing a cart on wheels or a walker.
27. Activity is individual rather than cooperative, but he "gets along " with other children.
28. Eats things like biscuit or bread holding in his own hand or uses spoon to eat from a bow, a cup, or a plate.
35. By actions or speech expresses to go to urinate or care himself; may be assisted at the same.
36. Occupies self at play such as drawing or colouring with pencil, looking at books or pictures.
41. Comes in out of rain. Shows some caution regarding strangers. Is careful as regards falling on stairs.
44. Gives simple accounts of experience or tells stories.
46. Participates in coordinated group activity as kindergarten circle games, cooking or group play.

49. Entertains others by reciting, singing, or dancing.
55. Draws forms like man, house, tree, animal etc.
56. Engages in tag, hide and seek, jumping, rope, tops, skipping, or marbles.
57. Hoops-ring pushed by hand or stick, cycle tyre.
59. Games with others requiring taking turns, observing rules without undue dissension; caroms, draft, snake, and ladder, trade etc.
60. Is responsible with small sums of money when sent to make payments of explicit purchases.
63. Writes (not prints) legibly with a pencil a dozen or more simple words with correct spelling.
65. Performs bedtime operation without help.; goes to room alone , changes dress and turns out-light.
67. After the meals is served first, helps himself more according to the need.
69. Boys: Games not requiring definite skill and with only less rules such as unorganised hockey, football, khokho and follow the leader. Takes hikes or bicycle rides.

    Girls: Engages in dramatic play symbolizing domestic or social situation such as playing house, school, doctor-nurses etc.,

    (Note: *Sex differentiation in play is noted at this stage and there is a shift in girls play to more sedentary ones. However, credit item regardless of sex if this differentiation has not yet been established.
71. Makes practical use of hammer, screwdriver and household articles. Sews. Uses garden tools etc.
72. Helps effectively at simple tasks for which some continuous responsibility is assumed; dusting; arranging; cleaning; washing dishes, making bed etc.
73. Reads comic strips, movie titles, simple stories, notes simple instructions, elementary news item for own entertainment or information.

76 Buys useful articles, exercises some choice or discretion in doing so and is responsible for safety of articles, money and correct change.

79. Able to decide for self, which shop to go for purchasing different articles.

80. Makes articles for self use, e.g. making simple gardens, stitching buttons, preparing tea for self, doing small repairs, talking care of own cabinet, table and room or performs occasional work on own initiative such as odd jobs, housework, helping in care of children, sewing, selling magazines, carrying newspapers for which some money is paid.

81. Writes letters to get information regarding some books, magazine or toys.

82. Makes useful articles; cooks, bakes, raises pets, writes simple stories or poems; produce simple drawings or painting.

83. Is sometimes left along and is successful in looking after own immediate needs or hose of others who may be left in his care.

85. Participates in skilled games and sports as card games, basketball, tennis, hockey, badminton, understands rules and methods of scoring.

86. Includes washing and drying hair, care of nails, proper selection of clothing according to occasion and weather.

87. Selects and purchases minor articles of personal clothing with regard for appropriateness, such as ribbons, underwear, linen, shoes etc.

88. Is an active member of a cooperative group, athletic team, club, social or literary organisation. Plans or participates in picnic trips, outdoor sports, etc.

89. Such as assisting in house work, caring for garden, cleaning car, washing window, waiting at table, bringing water etc.

VINELAND SOCIAL MATURITY SCALE—NORMS FOR PROFILE ANALYSIS

Maturity Levels (Years)	*Months*	*SHG*	*SHE*	*SHD*	*SD*	*OCC*	*COM*	*LOC*	*SOC*
	180					89			
XV	168				87				88
	156			86			84		85
	144				83	82			
XII	140								
	136								
	132					80	81		
XI	128				79				
	124								
	120								
X	116								
	112		75	74	76			77	
	108								
IX	104			70		72	73		
	100			70		71			
	96								69
VIII	92								
	88	66	67	65					68
	84			64					
VII	80						63		
	76		62					61	
	72								
VI	68				60				59
	64					57	58		56
	60			54		55			
V	56			52					
	52	51		50				53	
	48								
IV	44					48			49
	40			47			44	45	46
	36			42		43			
III	32	41	39	40		36			
	28	35	38	37					

(Contd...)

Maturity Levels (Years)	*Months*	*SHG*	*SHE*	*SHD*	*SD*	*OCC*	*COM*	*LOC*	*SOC*
	24.0		33				34		
	21.6	26	30			24	31	32	
II	19.2	23	28			22		29	27
	10.8		25	21		19	17	18	
	14.4		20						
	12.0	15							
	10.5	13							
	9.0	9	16			7	10	12	14
	7.5	8	11				1		4
I	6.0	6							
	4.5	5							
	3.0	3							
	1.5	2							

SHG-Self Help General
SHE-Self Help Eating
SHD-Self Help Dressing
SD-Self-Direction
OCC-Occupation
COM-Communication
LOC-Locomotion
SOC-Socialisation

VINELAND SOCIAL MATURITY SCALE
ANSWER AND SCORING SHEET

0-1 Year		**0-1 Year**			
1.	0.7 months	13.	9.1 months	24.	4.9 months
2.	1.4 months	14.	9.8 months	25.	5.6 months
3.	2.1 months	15.	10.6 months	26.	6.3 months
4.	2.8 months	16.	11.3 months	27.	7.0 months
5.	3.5 months	17.	12.0 months	28.	7.7 months
6.	4.2 months		**1 Year**	29.	8.4 months
7.	4.9 months	18.	0.7 months	30.	9.2 months
8.	5.6 months	19.	1.4 months	31.	9.9 months
9.	6.3 months	20.	2.1 months	32.	10.6 months
10.	7.0 months	21.	2.8 months	33.	11.3 months
11.	7.7 months	22.	3.5 months	34.	12.0 months
12.	8.4 months	23.	4.2 months		

(Contd...)

2 Years

35. 1.2 months
36. 2.4 months
37. 3.6 months
38. 4.8 months
39. 6.0 months
40. 7.2 months
41. 8.4 months
42. 9.6 months
43. 10.8 months
44. 12.0 months

3 Years

45. 2 months
46.. 4 months
47. 6 months
48. 8 months
49. 10 months
50. 12 months

4 Years

51. 2 months
52. 4 months
53. 6 months
54. 8 months
55. 10 months
56. 12 months

5 Years

57. 1.4 months
58. 4.8 months
59. 7.2 months
60. 9.6 months
61. 12.0 months

6 Years

62. 3 months
63. 6 months
64. 9 months
65. 12 months

7 Years

66. 2.4 months
67. 4.8 months
68. 7.2 months
69. 9.6 months
70. 12.0 months

8 Years

71. 3 months
72. 6 months
73. 9 months
74. 12 months

9 Years

75. 4 months
76. 8 months
77. 12 months

10 Years

78. 3 months
79. 6 months
80. 9 months
81. 12 months

11 Years

82. 4 months
83. 8 months
84. 12 months

12 Years

85. 7.2 months
86. 14.4 months
87. 21.6 months
88. 28.8 months
89. 36.0 months

Appendix—V

NIMH Development Screening Test

Name:			Number:
Date of Birth:			Date:
Sex: Male/Female			

S.No.	Developmental milestones	Pass: Yes/No	When achieved
1.	Head steady		
2.	Sits without support		
3.	Stands without support		
4.	Walks well		
5.	Smiles at others		
6.	Responds to name or voice		
7.	Talks in 2/3 words sentences		
8.	Tells name		
9.	Self feeding		
10.	Toilet control		

Note: Please ✓ if Passed

Please × is not passed.

Appendix—VI

Items for Behaviour Scale of AAMR

All the items grouped under 10 sub categories as given below, should rated as N, O or F (N-Never, O -Occasionally and F-Frequently)

1. VIOLENT BEHAVIOUR TOWARDS OTHERS

1. Threatens/Physical violence
2. Pushes others
3. Pinches others
4. Spits/smears saliva at others
5. Pulls hair/ear/body parts of others
6. Bites others
7. Kicks others
8. Hits/slaps others
9. Chokes others
10. Attacks with weapons
11. Throws objects at others
12. Pokes body parts of others

2. DESTRUCTIVE BEHAVIOURS

1. Tears/Pulls threads from clothing
2. Soils property (urination/defecation)
3. Tears up books/paper/magazines
4. Breaks objects/glass

5. Damages possessions/toys
6. Damages furniture
7. Damages personal belongings/other belongings/both

3. DISRUPTIVE BEHAVIOURS

1. Pulls objects from others
2. Does not allow others to carry on their own activities
3. Makes loud noises when others working/reading/ talking etc.
4. Takes other possessions without their permission
5. Crying excessively
6. Screaming/Yelling
7. Slamming doors
8. Banging objects
9. Stamping feet/Jumping up and down
10. Kicking legs while on floor rolling on floor.

    Situations when it is commonly observed:

4. SELF-INJURIOUS BEHAVIOURS

1. Head banging
2. Biting self
3. Cutting self
4. Pulling own hair
5. Picking at wounds on own body
6. Scratching/Rubbing self
7. Beating self
8. Putting objects into eyes/nose/ears
9. Eating food excessively
10. Eating unedible objects

5. REPETITIVE/STEREOTYPED BEHAVIOURS

1. Thumb sucking/putting fingers into mouth
2. Nail biting

3. Nose picking
4. Teeth grinding
5. Head nodding
6. Body rocking
7. Tapping feet continuously
8. Waving hands/Body parts continuously
9. Swinging round and round
10. Jumping up and down
11. Does the same activity over and again

6. ODD BEHAVIOURS

1. Laughs to self/laughs inappropriately
2. Talks to self loudly
3. Makes peculiar/unpleasant sounds
4. Mimics words (Echolalia)
5. Mimics gestures (Echopraxia)
6. Smears dirt/faeces on self
7. Plays with unacceptable objects excessively (Clothes, Chappals, string, faeces, water, dirt, etc.)
8. Hoarding unacceptable objects
9. Touching others unnecessarily
10. Standing close to people
11. Talking irrelevantly
12. Kisses/Hugs/Shakes hands/Licks people unnecessarily

7. ANTISOCIAL BEHAVIOURS

1. Lies
2. Steals
3. Makes obscene gestures
4. Undresses in front of others
5. Makes sexual overtures to members of the opposite sex

6. Gambling
7. Masturbation in front of others
8. Using vulgar/abusive language

8. WITHDRAWAL BEHAVIOURS

1. Sits/stands/lies down for long periods of time without doing anything.
2. No eye to eye contact
3. Does not talk spontaneously to others
4. Stares blankly
5. Does not give replies to questioning
6. Hides face in group situations
7. Sits with feet up/body curled up
8. Does not respond to calling by name even though hearing is normal
9. Avoids the company of people.

9. REBELLIOUS BEHAVIOURS

1. Refuses to follow (comply with) given instructions.
2. Breaks rules
3. Refuses to participate in regular activities at home/school/work
4. Refuses to perform regular routine on time (eating, waking, dressing, sleeping, etc.).
5. Refuses to attend to personal hygiene and self-care.
6. Does opposites of what is requested.
7. Refuses to pay attention when called/spoken to
8. Takes very long time intentionally to complete tasks.
9. Talks rudely/becomes argumentative

   Situations when it commonly served:

10. HYPERACTIVE BEHAVIOURS

1. Talking excessively
2. Wandering away from home/school
3. Pulling objects around him and missing the place.
4. Pacing up and down/running about the place.
5. Inability to sit at a place for 5 minutes continuously.

Index

K

L

M

N

O

P

R

S

T

U

V

W

Y